THE TRUTH
SHALL MAKE YOU
Odd

THE TRUTH SHALL MAKE YOU
Odd

Speaking with Pastoral Integrity
in Awkward Situations

Frank G. Honeycutt

BrazosPress
a division of Baker Publishing Group
Grand Rapids, Michigan

Published by Brazos Press
a division of Baker Publishing Group
P.O. Box 6287, Grand Rapids, MI 49516-6287
www.brazospress.com

Printed in the United States of America

Library of Congress Cataloging-in-Publication Data
Honeycutt, Frank G., 1957–
     The truth shall make you odd : speaking with pastoral integrity in awkward
  situations / Frank G. Honeycutt.
        p.   cm.
     Includes bibliographical references (p.   ).
     ISBN 978-1-58743-263-7 (pbk.)
     1. Pastoral theology. 2. Truthfulness and falsehood—Religious aspects—
  Christianity. I. Title.
  BV4013.H66 2010
  253—dc22   2010025333

11   12   13   14   15   16   17   7   6   5   4   3   2   1

For the Race and Reconciliation Group
of Columbia, South Carolina—
speaking truth in love to one another in the city
since January 2006:

Josh Lorick
Paul Pingel
Jesse Washington
Herman Yoos
Bob Johnson
Mary Anderson
James Grate
John Dooley
Joiquim Barnes
Preston Winkler
Henry Cleare

Contents

Acknowledgments

Many thanks to the people of Ebenezer Lutheran Church in Columbia, South Carolina, and our Congregation Council, who granted me a generous sabbatical during the summer of 2009 during which I wrote much of this book. The congregation has served faithfully in the city since 1830 (www .ebenezerlutheran.org).

For essentially handing me the key to their mountain cabin in Maggie Valley, North Carolina, I'm grateful to the ever-hospitable Sandy and Rich Roberson.

Thanks to the following folk who read portions of the early stages of the manuscript and offered valuable input and advice: John Hoffmeyer, Ed Davis, John Gifford, Larry Harley, Michael Kohn, Howard Pillot, Wayne Kannaday, Lee Honeycutt, Ron Luckey, and Douglass Sullivan-Gonzalez.

I'm grateful for many lay and clergy preachers who delivered excellent sermons in my absence: Ted Swanson, Matthew Titus, Karen Hardy, James Thomas, Marcus Miller, Harold Park, Ann Kelly, Dee Watson, David Donges, Michael Jeffcoat, and John Dooley.

Thanks also to our excellent church staff: Ken Robbins, Tom White, Wendy Isgett, James Grate, Amy Rollings, Paul Pingel, Diane Oliver, and Jami Sprankle.

Any book of this nature would be boring indeed without personal anecdotes and illustrations. In all cases, I've changed names, secured permission, and maintained strict pastoral confidentiality. You may see your own story in these pages. Know that your situation may be common to a number of other parishioners of my acquaintance.

As always, I'm filled with surprise, wonder, love, and thanksgiving for Cindy, Hannah, Marta, and Lukas Honeycutt, who gracefully tolerate my various idiosyncrasies, odd ways, and flawed intentions.

Introduction

Quivering Masses of Availability

It was not until after Dr. Myer's nurse, Polly, weighed me and rolled up the blood pressure cuff that I happened to remember that my absentminded underwear choice for that Tuesday morning—fished out in the dark from the big laundry basket at the end of our bed—was a rather shocking shade of scarlet.

It's hard to find basic white anymore in the men's stores in our town. My wife's Victoria's Secret catalogs arrive in the afternoon mail with every color choice imaginable. Men's briefs have followed suit, apparently. My tattered white hip-huggers, destined now for the ragbag but easily pressed into service to mop up stubborn kitchen spills, have been difficult to replace.

Lithe, plastic male models, so eternally self-assured with their flat abdomens and confident smiles, grace the Belk's department store display and seem prepared for any social situation—power lunch? the first tee?—wearing only fuchsia. I finally relented last month and purchased two multicolored three packs from the teenage girl behind the counter, who now knows more about me, a pastor entering his sixth decade, than I am honestly comfortable having her know. She offered more than the normal amount of smiling courtesy upon handing me a bag filled with male unmentionables, each more vibrant than Noah's famous rainbow.

"You'll need to strip down to your underwear now. The doctor will be in to see you in a moment," Polly declares professionally, breezing out into the hallway and securely shutting the door.

A minister is trained—through weary years of listening—to keep the pastoral antennae up, to work a room full of people without drawing personal attention, ever on the lookout for subtle spiritual swings and changes in the emotional barometers of others. Except when stepping into a pulpit, or raising chalice and paten at the Eucharist (wearing the colorful chasuble that hides a lot), I am largely invisible. I am typically a container for the concerns of others, and that is my preferred social posture. I listen and nod, making eye contact for long blocks of uninterrupted time. I'm a willing vessel into which woes and anxieties are poured.

Nothing surprises me anymore. With Qoheleth, I concur that there is not much new under the sun (Eccles. 1:9). And yet, as I undress, there is the nagging feeling that the doctor will detect in me some hidden illness uncharted in his medical books and I will finally make it onto my congregation's prayer list. Contemplating such a prospect, I redden.

My black clerical shirt with matching white-tab collar hangs loosely on a chair. I look around the bare room and read the doctor's diplomas. Credentials comfort me. The crinkling surface of the examining table reminds me of Christmas morning and the sounds of wrapping paper my brothers and I used to toss around the tree as children.

How had I overlooked this possibility—an overworked and rather serious man of the cloth sitting in a stark room wearing what seems the equivalent of a bull's-eye painted on his crotch? Will the doctor see this colorful undergarment as some sort of cryptic sign? Perhaps of a pastor at peace with himself, shamelessly offering a confident gender statement? I am comfortable in my south-sliding flesh, but this situation seems to cry out for someone's skillful exegesis. I wonder who will speak first to interrupt the silence.

I usually bring work to distract me from the chill of this room, but today I've forgotten to do so, having left my briefcase in the car. Listening closely for the familiar rustle of medical papers just outside the door, I recall my mother's odd 1964 indulgence of her then seven-year-old son. In those early years she allowed me to pee into a small Mason jar, tightly screw on the security lid, and bury the whole operation in a shallow hole. Don't ask me why I did this, why she allowed it, or how many jars I buried in the backyard.

Well into adulthood, I asked Mom if she had any recollection of my burial ritual and what it might have meant. She only smiled and laughed softly. The prophet Jeremiah once buried his underwear (Jer. 13:1–11) near a river (and then dug it up for examination, unlaundered) to symbolize national faithlessness and fickleness in obedience to the commands of the living God. So if my strange actions do prove symbolic of something big, they may put me in fairly good company.

Once when Jesus's family became convinced he'd gone over the deep end, they came looking for him, interrupting his public lecture and trying to take him away (Mark 3:21). I say a private prayer thanking God for the understanding family that gave birth to me, such a complicated cleric. But I wonder fleetingly if Dr. Myer has somehow gathered early urinary information from my secret source and if it, coupled with the vivid shorts, will be enough to make him inquire about pastoral stress these days.

There are steps in the hallway and a quiet knock. Polly peeks in and reports that the doctor is on his way. It's unclear from her expression whether she notices what I'm wearing. Would her reaction or Dr. Myer's matter more? Should I tell him right up front, with a quick laugh even before the handshake, that I would have never worn red had I remembered my appointment upon stepping out of the shower?

The door swings open and the physician enters. "So how've you been, pastor? Hey, nice shorts!"

"Thanks," I reply. "I knew you'd appreciate them."

• • •

The book you are holding is written for pastors like me, often a quivering mass of availability,[1] who sometimes struggle with telling the truth, half-truths, and even downright lies. Truth telling is an ancient struggle within the hearts of clergy and among those with whom we are called to serve. Our Lord was right: "For it is from within, from the human heart, that evil intentions come" (Mark 7:21). Our human hearts can be deceptive and artful in their attempts to prevent Jesus from doing business with our unfiltered inner lives.[2] The good news is that Jesus is relentless about breaking in with a light that shines in the darkness and cannot be overcome (John 1:5).

In the pages that follow, I will examine a variety of ministerial contexts in which clergy truth telling is essential for congregational health. In short, when and how does a pastor speak the truth in love (Eph. 4:15) no matter the cost or congregational fallout? Maslow and his hierarchy of needs listed *identity* as a critical component in emotional health. When pastoral identity is centered upon pleasing people (rather than Jesus), our ability to speak and live the truth of the gospel is severely crippled. It's easy to settle for half-truths and this or that religious bromide, a bone of gospel sweetness tossed to people who need much more. If you've ever almost gagged at the artificiality of some funerals, you'll know what I mean.

Many pastors, including myself, spend far too much time reflecting on what others think of us. How will this sermon be received? What will people think if I take this particular stand on the war? On capital punishment? On anything at all? What should I say to this divorcing couple whose marriage might be saved with some effort? How can I offer honest yet potentially alienating words to parents who may never show up again after their child's baptism day?

I've been a pastor for twenty-five years. This book is mainly written for clergy and seminarians just learning about the ancient craft of leading a congregation. I will discuss my own mistakes, flaws, and painful truths, and I suspect you'll see some of your own experiences in them. Lay folk and study groups will also benefit from this book as they seek to understand the unique tasks of pastoral ministry in a climate in which clergy are often expected to be "nice and affirming." A church committee just starting a call process might read this book to gain more clarity about why Jesus sends pastors to congregations in the first place. Or a pastoral support committee could use it to better understand the behind-the-scenes issues that sometimes contribute to a pastor's early exit. But this book is centrally for pastors like me as we ponder the odd nature of our call from a surpassingly odd Lord.

Emily Dickinson said in one of her poems, "Tell all the truth, but tell it slant." What she meant (at least in part) is that unedited truth can sometimes completely crush and overwhelm a person. "Truthful statements," writes Sissela Bok, "though they are not meant to deceive, can, of course, themselves be coercive and destructive; they can be used as weapons, to wound and do violence."[3] Pastors often need to tell the truth in creative ways—in the pulpit, in a counseling session, in the classroom—so that the ways of Jesus creep up on and even surprise people in manageable doses they can assimilate and understand. Many sermons attempt to pound the truth into captive listeners. And there is indeed a time and place for pronouncements of "thus sayeth the Lord." But Jesus more often taught and preached this Dickinsonian slanted way—with parables that still detonate in the lives of listeners long after they were first heard.

Before tackling specific ministry areas, I will examine the liturgical power of baptismal renunciation of the devil (the Father of Lies). In a companion chapter, I'll turn to the importance of developing a local process of adult Christian conversion. After five chapters addressing areas where pastors spend most of our time, I will make a concluding case as to why church parishioners need more than care in order to grow in Christian discipleship.

Much of what you will find written here is difficult, comes with inherent risk attached, and may make people angry enough to create relational fallout that requires a great deal of pastoral time to sort out. It's a whole lot easier to remain quiet in parish life—to adopt the role of the kind and easygoing chaplain who never offends—and to count the years until retirement. Even while writing these words, I'm thinking of several people who've left congregations I've served, furious with Christ's truthful Word offered through the mouth of their pastor. Saint Paul asks of the church in Galatia, "Have I now become your enemy by telling you the truth?" (Gal. 4:16). One parishioner stormed out of my office many years ago with the words, "I thought you were here to serve this parish!" It's a common confusion. The parish indeed calls a pastor. But we serve Jesus, always Jesus, for the sake and health of the people of God.

Wrote the great nineteenth-century preacher C. H. Spurgeon, "I have tried, especially of late, to take no more notice of man's praise than of his blame."[4] That's an enviable place from which to do pastoral work. Pastoral nature is generally inclined toward wanting to please others. Many of us unconsciously enter seminary with that as part of our personality profile. Pastors would do well to forever remember the words of Balaam, who came to his senses after being confronted by a talking ass and a sword-wielding angel in the book of Numbers. "Do I have the power to say just anything?" Balaam addresses those who want him to speak in partisan half-truths. "The word God puts in my mouth—*that* is what I must say" (Num. 22:38).

● ● ●

The title of this book is taken from a quote attributed to Flannery O'Connor, the late southern fiction writer. She was fond of paraphrasing Jesus's claims about truth telling in John 8:32 thusly: "You shall know the truth, and the truth shall make you *odd*" (italics mine). The truth offered by Jesus is indeed liberating, but living that truth will also create people who are out of step, unusual, and downright strange. If pastors and churches are not feeling some of this strangeness on a regular basis, we have probably relegated Jesus to a realm that has little to do with the daily realities of this life.

Martin Luther once likened preaching to surgery. Most people are not naturally inclined toward surgery, even when they know it's the best route. Telling the truth in a culture of deceit and lies is exhausting but ultimately healing work. We need the honest Great Physician, even if he tells us things we don't want to hear.

● ● ●

I've written much of this book while on sabbatical, my third in twenty-five years of ministry. Sabbaticals are wonderfully refreshing. Many pastors are exhausted, calling out for refreshment, running hither and yon to satisfy everyone's needs. Some do this too long and end up leaving the ministry entirely. I'm convinced the church is shooting its collective self in the foot when it doesn't afford pastors a break. Why can't bishops work with call committees and say something like, "In seven years a pastor works twenty-eight quarters of God's holy time. Those seven years are actually more like nine years of regular work if you add up all the hours. We're going to ask pastors to work hard and faithfully for twenty-seven quarters. On the twenty-eighth, they stop. They get a sabbatical. If you don't like this new policy, I won't send you any more potential candidates for your pastoral vacancy. Call me when you're ready to talk some more."

But even bishops are prone to embody the Stanley Hauerwas maxim. Clergy have been trained to be "quivering masses of availability." Or maybe they arrived quivering on a seminary campus. We all like to please people. Trouble is, we often try to please people who don't want what Jesus wants. That's a toxic mix.

There's a time and a place for unedited truth. But how do we know when to be truthfully blunt and when to be artfully truthful? How do we know when to be Jeremiah and when to be Nathan? They were both very faithful prophets.

Our challenge in any century is to learn how to speak Jesus's truth. What does it mean to tell the truth, the whole truth, and nothing but the truth about Jesus in pastoral ministry? How in the world did he do it? Was that part of what got him killed only three years into it?

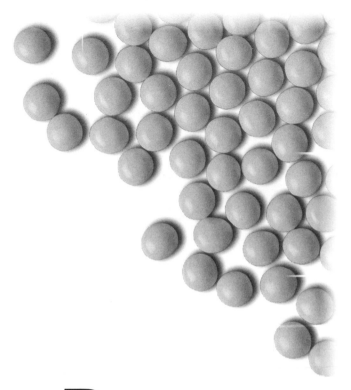

PART 1

1

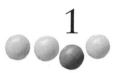

Reflections on the Father of Lies

The Devil and All His Empty Promises

I write to you, not because you do not know the truth, but because you know it, and you know that no lie comes from the truth.

1 John 2:21

If, like truth, the lie had but one face, we would be on better terms. For we would accept as certain the opposite of what the liar would say. But the reverse of truth has a hundred thousand faces and an infinite field.[1]

Sissela Bok

He was a murderer from the beginning and does not stand in the truth, because there is no truth in him. When he lies, he speaks according to his own nature, for he is a liar and the father of lies.

John 8:44

Somebody called the church office a couple weeks ago and asked if we did exorcisms here at Ebenezer Lutheran. Our secretary said, "Well, no, I can't recall the last one." "Thank you," said the caller. "I'll try another church."

As a teenager, I saw Linda Blair's young head spin around 360 degrees in *The Exorcist*. I heard the odd voices, watched the projectile vomiting splattering the priest, and all that. It spooked me—and countless others of my generation. I enjoyed little sleep for days.

In the sixteenth century, Martin Luther wrote how he was troubled by evil spirits in the days before and during his public confrontation of the Roman church hierarchy. Luther was torn between faithfulness to the church and faithfulness to Christ. Sparks flew. Was the poor guy just suffering from lack of sleep and prone to psychological fantasies? He later famously threw an inkwell at a palpable demonic voice in Wartburg Castle. Some say you can still see the stain on the wall. In his famous hymn, "A Mighty Fortress," Luther writes, "One little word subdues him." And who is "him"? Well, the devil, of course—Satan, "the father of lies" (John 8:44). Was Luther naive in such belief? Was he the brilliant theological product of a now outdated worldview?

The Reality of Satan

Do we believe in the demonic? Evil spirits? Or do we write off all strange behavior to the sliver of popular culture obsessed with bizarre, paranormal tabloid headlines, sensational movies like the *Saw* series, and numerous television shows produced for the misguided and bored masses?

My favorite Carl Hiaasen novel, *Skinny Dip*, includes a loveable but definitely unbalanced fellow named Tool. He careens around southwest Florida stealing entire highway fatality shrines from roadside places of mourning. Tool plants them in his backyard "in place of vegetables," presumably to ward off his own very real and personal demons.

> The small homemade crosses often displayed colorful floral arrangements, which Tool found pleasing to the eye. Whenever he spied one of the markers along a road, he would yank it from the ground and place it in the back of his truck. Often this act was witnessed by other motorists, though nobody ever attempted to interfere. Tool stood six three and weighed 280 pounds and owned a head like a cinder block. . . . Nearly a year had passed since Tool had been shot in broad daylight by a poacher who had mistaken him for a bear.[2]

In the *Lutheran* magazine (ELCA) several years ago, a reader survey[3] found that while a large majority of respondents believe unequivocally in God and heaven, a much smaller percentage of the same respondents believe in the devil, hell, and evil forces. "It's all good" is a well-known slogan offered by many upbeat Christians. Jesus may have descended into hell, claims the Apostles' Creed, but that was then and this is now. Belief in hell and the devil is often reserved for marginally sane folk like Tool.

The danger of any serious theological demon-talk is that it's a very slippery slope to concluding that our enemies (personal and national) are all in league with the devil. Pretty soon we've named our own personal Axis of Evil at the workplace, in our politics, even in our close relationships. A character in a Tobias Wolff short story, reflecting on the devil, comes to realize "there were certain priests who cast out demons as a specialty. That was their job, their market niche, waiting around like firemen for the alarm to go off. Demon in Idaho housewife! Demon in Delaware bus driver! How weird was that? As if being a priest weren't strange enough already."[4]

But there's another, contrasting danger in going the way of the large majority in the *Lutheran*'s survey. One writer, reflecting on the atrocities of the world and how humans treat one another, puts it this way: "The repertoire of evil," he says, "has never been richer. Yet never have our [theological] responses been so weak. We have no language for connecting our inner lives with the horrors that pass before our eyes in the outer world. . . . We have an inescapable problem: we feel something that our culture no longer gives us the vocabulary to express."[5] That quote, tellingly, is from a book titled *The Death of Satan*.

What Have You to Do with Us?

In the Gospel of Mark, there is no Christmas story—no wise men, no shepherds, no angelic host. Jesus appears on the scene, he's quickly baptized, and the Bible then says the Holy Spirit "immediately drove him out into the wilderness" to go at it with the devil for forty days. That "drove him out" is an odd choice of words, if you ask me. It was not a polite suggestion by the Spirit. Jesus hardly has time to towel off and then, *zoom*, the spirit drives him out toward a titanic encounter between good and evil. The proximity of the two events suggests that baptism is not some sweet splash of inoculation that protects us from evil and mishap. In Jesus's case, baptism does not protect him from evil; it instead hastens his encounter with it.

Though our belief in evil appears to have waned, many of our baptismal liturgies still include a jarring renunciation of "the devil and all his many promises." I once asked my theology professor in seminary, Michael Root, if I really had to say that line. I was intellectually embarrassed by the words. Dr. Root said, "Spend twenty years in parish ministry and come back and ask me that again." I haven't needed to.

Still damp, Jesus is driven into the desert only twelve verses into the Gospel of Mark. Then, after he chooses two sets of brothers to be his first disciples, together they hike down to Capernaum, a little town perched on the edge of the sea. He doesn't bless anybody there. He doesn't dangle children on his knee in a field of tulips. He doesn't coddle the four disciples and tell them what great guys they are for assenting to his odd invitation even though they've just met. Instead, Jesus enters a synagogue and teaches (Mark 1:21–28). Never underestimate the power of teaching. I'm sure you could name two or three teachers who literally changed your life.[6]

What's doubly interesting is that the demons in this worship assembly—let's just call it church, even though there are obvious differences between church and synagogue—do not emerge *until* Jesus starts teaching. His teaching seems to flush them out. Our Lord does not first encounter evil in any number of obviously shady places: a drug den, a bordello, or some gathering of thieves. No, Jesus initially encounters evil in a church setting. That's both curious and amusing, especially since churches (and pastors like me) are often so prone to point out evil in a variety of places away from church. *We're* the holy ones, right? Yet Jesus starts to teach in church and out come the demons, maybe ruining the new flooring and wrecking the walls.

And boy, are these demons ever chatty. *What have you to do with us? Have you come to destroy us? I know who you are.* They sound like a bunch of gossipy middle schoolers. Bank on this: Jesus is going to be resisted. Jesus will be resisted even in church. Jesus will be resisted by pastors and lay leaders. Jesus will be resisted by me.

Why in the world would I want to resist such a swell guy? Because it's in my best interest to do so. Jesus came into this world to change me. And to be honest, I really don't like to change. Jesus didn't come to hold my hand. He didn't come to fit into my schedule. He didn't come to affirm and coddle me. He might receive me "Just As I Am," as the old hymn puts it, but he sure doesn't intend to leave me that way. "What have you to do with us, Jesus?" It's a pretty good question offered by the demons. Here's another: *what have you to do with me?*

Evil Close to Home

In a wonderfully imagined novel, *The Testament of Gideon Mack*, a Scottish Presbyterian pastor finally confesses to himself that he believes nothing at all—no God, nothing. Reverend Gideon Mack's work focuses mainly on raising money for pet outreach projects in his little town. It's difficult to distinguish this work from the local equivalent of the United Way. Gideon continues his work as a pastor and preaches tolerable sermons until he falls into a river trying to rescue a friend's dog. The tired and cynical pastor sinks far below the water's surface. After almost drowning (ponder the baptismal connections and read Rom. 6:1–11), he's rescued in a dark underworld by the devil. Assisting Gideon with new but grungy clothing around a fire (he's been stripped naked by the force of the water), the devil responds to the pastor's doubt that he is real:

> What do you want me to do, show you a cloven hoof? Horns in my head, a forky tail and live coals for eyes? Is that what you want? Do you want me to take you up some mountain and show you my empire? Make loaves out of these stones? . . . I can do all of those things. . . . Do you want me to show you my supposed greatest achievement? Battlefields, wars, torture chambers, famines, plagues . . . mass murders? I can do that too, but what's the point? You know it all already and you don't believe I'm responsible for it. So what is it you want

me to prove? That I exist? Look, here I am. Do you think I'm doing this for fun?[7]

The devil in this provocative tale is a dejected and rather sad figure, actually a lot like Gideon. "I like the way you deal with religion. One century you're up to your lugs in it, the next you're trading the whole apparatus in for Sunday superstores," this devil remarks of Gideon and his kind.[8] As a true wreaker of havoc, the devil's day is in the past.

> I used to have a purpose. We both had a purpose, God and me. Now? I just go from one window to another and stare out. Or stare in. Sometimes I do a few conjuring tricks, push a button here, pull a lever there. But my heart's not in it. Basically, I don't do anything any more. I despair, if you want the honest truth. I mean, the world doesn't need me. It's going to hell on a handcart, if you'll excuse the cliché, without any assistance from me.[9]

I don't know what you really believe about the devil, demons, and evil in the world today. I suspect we're all (including pastors) a bit naive about these matters. And if we do believe in such forces, we usually locate them in dark, sinister places halfway across the world or in somebody else's life—certainly not in ours.

Luke 13:1–9 illustrates this last point precisely, though bizarrely. Here Jesus trots out two local news stories— planned evil and natural catastrophe—to make a wider point about personal repentance. For my money the report of mass murder and a collapsing tower has to rank right up there among the top five strange teachings ever uttered by Jesus. It may just win the blue ribbon of oddness. The story appears only in Luke, and I cite it here because the exchange between Jesus and his disciples ultimately exposes evil inside the church rather than outside, thus underscoring our great need for renunciation and a baptismal rite that takes evil seriously, using ancient sacramental language without apology.

Far too often pastors like me politely indulge in the common fallacy that baptism somehow inoculates Christians against any real encounter with whatever may be "out there." Doing so facilitates all our easy lies about sin and death. Why should we now be surprised that baptism seems like nothing more than an obligation to many nominal Christians? And why do pastors sometimes allow marginally active parishioners to dictate how, when, where, and on whose terms baptism will take place?

To test whether you've really sensed the oddness of this strange story from Luke's pen, compare it to a news report that appeared in the *New York Times*. "The book market along Mutanabi Street was a throwback to the Baghdad of old, students browsing for texts, turbaned clerics hunting down religious tomes, and café intellectuals debating politics over backgammon. Somehow it had survived the war—until Monday, when a powerful suicide bomb hit the market, slicing through the heart of the capital's intellectual scene. It killed at least 20 people and wounded more than 65."[10]

Now plant yourself in Luke 13:1–9 as one of Jesus's disciples. You might ask Jesus, "Those twenty people who were killed over in the book market, surely they weren't worse sinners than anyone else living in Baghdad, were they?" There is a brief pause as Jesus ponders the question. You breathe a sigh of relief as our Lord replies, "Heavens no, get that crazy idea out of your head, will you? Just because something horrible happens to a person doesn't mean he's done something sinister to deserve it." In Jesus's day, there was an assumed theological cause and effect connection between suffering and sin. You may recall that when Job is afflicted with a series of calamities, companions urge him to confess the things he's done to bring all these calamities upon himself. To Job's credit, he angrily refuses. I also think of the question posed by the disciples of Jesus: "Rabbi, who sinned, this man or his parents, that he was born blind?" (John 9:2). And so an alert reader of Luke 13 breathes a sigh of relief. "No," says Jesus. "Come on now, stuff happens. These poor people are no worse sinners than anybody else."

But Jesus doesn't stop there, does he? He looks directly at these disciples and says, "But unless you repent, your future doesn't look so bright. Unless you repent, you will perish just like these unfortunate people in the Baghdad book market."

Am I getting the details about right here? In Luke's odd theological twist, one reads of two horrible happenings that would have easily made the evening news. One was hatched and calculated evil by a political despot, Pilate. The other event was what insurance people still call "an act of God," in this case the collapse of a tower. Some unlucky people just got in the way. And here Jesus again reacts in much the same way. "No, the tower falling doesn't mean the poor people under it did anything wrong. Stop it with such shoddy theology. But keep your eyes open during the next vacation you may take near a fault line. Because unless you repent, a collapsing building is in your own future."

These two news events from Luke pretty much cover the waterfront of woe that we hear about on a daily basis—tragedy planned by horrible people or tragedy that happens because somebody got in the way of the weather or some accidental occurrence. Thank God, in both cases, that Jesus refuses to play along with the conventional wisdom of his day. Neither of these events befell the victims because of past behavior. I like Jesus here. I'm cheering for him.

But then he turns and looks at the crowd (he looks at me) and suggests that similar tragedy is in my own future unless I repent. I feel like I'm on a theological roller coaster. As God reports in the book of Isaiah, "My thoughts are not your thoughts, nor are your ways my ways" (55:8). No argument here about that.

We live in a society that is absolutely saturated, even drowning, in news. I invite you to take a media break. Turn off the constant blather of tragedy peppered with happy commercials about the "goodness of maize." Here's something I've noticed about tragic news. It lets me off the hook. I hear about a tragedy. I learn about sadness or evil malice. And very often, here's my internal response: "I'm not a perfect person. I may have my own share of flaws, but you know what? At least I'm not as screwed up or as woeful as these other people."

That last sentence is precisely why I think Jesus throws a repentance curveball in this odd lesson from Luke. The woes of this life can distract me from my own sin and from my own complicity in remaining silent in the face of suffering. The never-ending parade of tragedies piped into our homes assures us that our own little indiscretions are really not that bad and fuels indifference to the plight of others whose figurative and real towers are collapsing. In a poem by R. T. Smith, the narrator concludes, "What do you think evil is if not the lack of sympathy?"[11]

It was interesting to follow the dark community reaction to a massive wildfire just after the scorching of the Myrtle Beach area in April of 2009. You can't make this stuff up. It's right out of Genesis 2–3. The old blame game lives on:

> The man being fined for setting the yard fire that started the wildfire said the county firefighters who responded twice last Saturday to his small blaze should take the blame, not him. He wondered how he could be faulted for the fire re-igniting

Wednesday, when it began a raging trek along the coast destroying homes, most located about ten miles from his home. "It was four days later," said Marc Torchi,[12] a 39-year-old landscaper. "How can they even come up with something like that?" Torchi's wife said the family has received death threats since officials announced he would be fined for the yard fire and linked it to the state's largest wildfire in more than three decades."[13]

In C. S. Lewis's fictional classic *The Screwtape Letters*, Uncle Screwtape gives sound and diabolical advice to help turn a potential disciple of Christ away from any need to confess personal sin and wrongdoing. "You must bring him to a condition in which he can practice self-examination for an hour without discovering any of those facts about himself which are perfectly clear to anyone who has ever lived in the same house with him or worked in the same office."[14]

Through the upside-down logic of Lewis's tormentors, we see Jesus's ability to call a bluff. When I welcome his revelation, he will not allow me to be diverted from the facts about myself. He wants to know how it is with me, Frank Honeycutt, and God. He will not indulge me in a comparison of my mundane flaws to the flamboyant flaws of others. "Unless *you* repent," he says. The tragic stories we hear each day often only divert us from the hard work of personal repentance to which baptism (and renunciation) calls us over and again.

So if the struggle against the powers of darkness is real; if we are not protected from "the devil and all his empty promises"[15] just because Christians show up and mumble the Apostles' Creed with various degrees of regularity; if indeed the conflict may be heightened and hastened (Mark 1:12–13) due to baptism itself; and if this devil is not nearly as obvious as popular culture paints him or her in the myriad temptations dished out all around us, what in the world are

11

we to use as resources in this struggle? Our good intentions? Intestinal fortitude? Common sense? A Ouija board?

It's instructive to discover how Jesus overcomes specific temptations of personal power, fame, and immediate gratification. He quotes Scripture (Matt. 4:1–11) and grounds himself in an old tradition that predates the latest psychological "explanations" for evil in the world. In short, he sasses the devil with the Word.

Renunciation of Evil

In early Christian baptism, the rite sometimes involved removal of clothing and jewelry before immersion in the waters. At the Great Vigil of Easter, candidates turned toward the west and darkness before the rising of the sun (Son) in the east. Some liturgies include an actual spitting at the devil before those baptized were plunged into the water.[16] Cyril of Jerusalem (350–87 CE) writes:

> When you renounce Satan, you trample underfoot your entire covenant with him, and abrogate your former treaty with hell. The Gates of God's Paradise are open to you, the garden which God planted in the east, and from which our first parent was expelled for his transgression. When you turned from west to east, the region of light, you symbolized the change of allegiance.[17]

The period leading up to baptism (which became our Lent) was often filled with a series of rites known as "scrutinies." Sometimes they amounted to a sort of exorcism involving the candidates for the sacrament. We've largely given up such drama, retaining only the vestiges of renunciation in modern liturgies.

The late Scott Peck, perhaps best known for his book *The Road Less Traveled*, has another, lesser known book in which he describes satanic possession and attending actual exorcisms, one of which "turned out to be the real thing."[18] Peck (by vocation a psychotherapist) admits that actual satanic possession as we see it in the movies is relatively rare, but his observation struck me:

> In my experience, all good psychotherapy does in fact combat lies. . . . Exorcism is another matter. Here the healer calls every power that is legitimately, lovingly available in the battle against the patient's sickness. . . . Indeed, as far as the Christian exorcist is concerned, it is not he or she who successfully completes the process; it is God who does the healing. The whole purpose of the prayer and the ritual is to bring the power of God into the fray.[19]

That's oddly comforting in a way. With most garden-variety possession in church life, pastors are only dealing with liars. No need to break out the big guns—nice to know that. But that's also the challenge of pastoral life. We tend to overlook lies and half-truths in other people (and also in ourselves). The Bible, however, suggests there is indeed a father of all deception. And whether you're Jeffrey Dahmer or Frank Honeycutt, big and little lies sprout from the same soil.

I've started visiting a man on death row in lower South Carolina. Though our situations are different in many ways, I've been able to find common ground with this man—even laughter. We've discovered common sin and very familiar flaws in each other. "Everyone is a liar" (Rom. 3:4). Lie often enough and artfully enough and God suddenly seems expendable, replaceable. It's an old story. Promises the deceptive serpent in Genesis, "You will not die; for God knows that when you eat of it your eyes will be opened, and you will be like God, knowing good and evil" (3:4–5). I'm afraid that the serpent was lying, because I've danced and eaten around

13

the old tree all my life and I still can't consistently tell the difference between the former and the latter.

• • •

The story from Mark's opening chapter should unsettle us. Demons show up in church, for Pete's sake, among good people like you and me. So the church is no holy haven of protection and goodness. We're not the church because we're such special, righteous people. I think we know better than that. We all struggle with personal demons—past and present.

"Have you come to destroy us?" the demons ask of Jesus.

In a word, yes. Precisely. Jesus comes to destroy individualism and build community. He comes to destroy our biases and convert us slowly into his image. He comes to destroy our ideas about religion and to birth the church. He comes to destroy our lies.

A Brief Excursus on Angelic Tardiness

There is a rather odd story in the book of Daniel (10:10–14) concerning an angel who is running late, twenty-one days late.[20] Stranded in Babylon, exiled and far from home, it's tough to keep the faith. So Daniel, in a jam, prays for help. He receives absolutely no hint that his prayer has been heard. For me, Daniel is a poster child for those who've tried to pray with little "success." There is no initial evidence that Daniel's efforts are anything more than wishful thinking offered into a vast void.

Divine assistance finally does show up in Daniel's apartment, but the tardiness requires an explanation. Why the long discrepancy between human prayer and angelic arrival? The excuse offered by the angel seems almost comical. The lag time between intercession and response is due to a wrestling match of cosmic proportions between the tardy angel and an evil prince of darkness who hails from Persia. For twenty-one days (v. 13) these two wrestling foes grunt and sweat until Saint Michael jumps into the ring (the first tag team?) and frees the unnamed angel long enough for him to swoop into Daniel's den with an explanation of his delay. "From the first day that you set your mind to gain understanding and to humble yourself before your God, your words have been heard, and I have come because of your words" (v. 12). The angel seems to say, "Sorry, I wanted to arrive earlier, but I was tied up unavoidably with other matters you know nothing about."

Pastors engage in a variety of activities over the course of their careers. The oddness of their profession requires them to change gears a lot. I recall several months ago boarding an elevator on the seventh floor of a hospital in Columbia. I had just prayed with a woman who was dying. The elevator then took me down to the third floor where I celebrated with a couple that couldn't stop staring and smiling at their new baby. Only four floors and a couple of minutes separated my experiences with the two families, but the emotional distance between them was immense. E. M. Forster once said, "We move between two darknesses. The two entities who might enlighten us, the baby and the corpse, cannot do so."[21] I cannot think of another profession—medical, psychological, sociological—that experiences more barometric swings in exposure to such a variety of human situations than pastors. We are, in a word, odd.

Christians traffic in fantastic theological claims, none of which is more amazing than this: "We believe in one God, the Father, the Almighty, maker of heaven and earth, of all that is, seen and unseen." A pastor does a lot of things— some mundane, others profound. But all of it is bound up

15

in helping a congregation trust and make sense of an unseen realm breaking into this one. One of my favorite poets, Luci Shaw, has a great line in one of her poems: "It's a cracked, crossover world," she says, "waiting for bridges."[22] This is where pastors stand: in the middle of the bridge between seen and unseen, making sense of the traffic linking heaven and earth and helping others learn how to discern it. Traffic up and down, around and beyond, like the ladder of angels in Jacob's dream at Bethel (Gen. 28:10–17).

Said the tardy angel to Daniel, "I heard your prayers. I'm here precisely because of them. But I was tied up—held up in a cosmic struggle that you cannot see." To stand on that bridge and tell people that their prayers are often delayed for twenty-one days or twenty-one months or twenty-one years or even twenty-one centuries is no easy task. How we pray in the face of unanswered prayer reveals more about one's understanding of God than most anything else.

I heard an amazing story on National Public Radio recently. Melissa Block and Robert Siegel were reporting that more than one-half of the world's languages are expected to disappear by the end of the century—the eighty or so dominant languages squeezing out the weaker ones in places ranging from northern Australia to the Pacific Northwest in the United States.

The loss of so many languages so quickly seems a tragedy, but it also helps me realize that we are all engaged in a mission to make sure the strange and rather exotic language of the Christian faith is not lost over time—that it won't be squeezed out of the lives of parishioners and members of our churches. It's a new time, in many ways, for the church in North America. Talk seriously of angels and their tardiness and a vast unseen realm filled with demons and evil spirits, and you will be met with a chorus of loud hoots and guffaws by a growing number of folk both outside and within the church.

The story that we tell, this strange language we teach and transmit, has the power to form us into people who love justice, do kindness, walk humbly, and face death with confidence. When those first seventy evangelists returned with joy from their initial mission, Jesus said to them: "Nothing will hurt you" (Luke 10:19). Think of the implications of such a promise. *Nothing will hurt you.* If we have already died in baptism (Rom. 6:3; Col. 3:3), nothing can "get" us. On my best days, I believe that.

That's what a pastor, a church, devotes a life to—a language, a particular way, to words over time that confidently shape us into people who walk fearlessly into situations that seem extremely fearful and very strange. "Nothing will hurt you." We stand on the bridge between the cracked, crossover worlds and share the lovely and liberating language of Jesus— even (and perhaps especially) when the angels seem late. Church is the place where we learn the language of Jesus, a language faithfully spoken less and less frequently, even by pastors like me.

Gift and Liability: "I Can See the Future"

Multiple times[23] in the New Testament, the church is comforted with the reality of certain and lavish gifts of the Holy Spirit used to build up the church and combat the onslaught of the evil one (and cope with the seeming delay of any practical help). To be honest, most really effective spiritual gifts (any gift, actually) bestowed on us by God can also become a liability—warped and misshapen by the devil. For example, the devil's temptations in the wilderness do not look so bad at first glance. They actually look pretty good. All of the things

17

the devil waves under the nose of Jesus are not necessarily evil. Look at the list closely (Luke 4:1–13). The so-called temptations can each be turned toward good (or evil) ends.

For example, I can sometimes see the future clearly, anticipating certain inevitable outcomes, the natural unfolding of good and bad consequences. I can name the pitfalls, describing how decisions will lead naturally and inevitably from point A to point F. I see how to get to a desired destination quickly and efficiently.

That I jump ahead and believe I know what will happen can make me seem arrogant. I cut to the chase a lot, which pisses people off—whether it's my wife, who wants to talk through her feelings from a particularly trying day at school; my pastoral colleague, who is my exact opposite in personality type; or my daughter, who doesn't want to hear that she's following too closely to the car up ahead. Church members who want to discuss and process a problem, who want to talk about possible options and solutions and potential hurt feelings among the flock may feel frustrated with me. Don't people know Jesus was a man of action and not a handholder? He told the truth and let the chips fall where they may (Luke 13).

I'm not a fan of the Meyers–Briggs test, or the church's reliance on it, but I feel like the test is pretty accurate where I'm concerned. According to Meyers–Briggs, I'm an INTJ,[24] which means I have the gift to see way down the road and tell people how to get there quickly. My ability is also a liability. My children tell me I'm funny. They also tell me I'm a jerk sometimes, which is true. My aforementioned spouse says that in my case the *T* in INTJ often stands for *turd*. I love her for her honesty.

Anyway, the devil can use all this, can twist and misshape an ability into a liability and make us think all bad behavior is a different and needed reflection of the same "gift" from God. I recently discovered that our local University of South Carolina has what's interestingly called the Center for Deception.[25] Its goal is to discover what makes people lie. Strangely enough, the church itself sometimes serves as the Center for Deception for the devil and "all his empty promises." We can sometimes be deceived into believing that our own hurtful behavior is nothing more than "the way God made us," and the path to real truth is sabotaged by every sort of personal justification of our sin. It's easy to arrive (often unconsciously) at the conclusion of Hazel Motes in Flannery O'Connor's *Wise Blood*: "I preach there are all kinds of truth, your truth and somebody else's, but behind all of them, there's only one truth and that is that there's no truth."[26]

Saint Paul once wrote, "But speaking the truth in love, we must grow up in every way into him who is the head, into Christ" (Eph. 4:15). An expectation of depth and maturity, truth *and* love, conversion involves both.[27] In the next chapter, I'll show you how we offer a process of adult Christian conversion where I serve in South Carolina. Conversion to Jesus, never fully complete or finished in any of us, is a project in dire need of reframing in the mainline church. Any authentic conversion process in a local congregation will unmask our penchant for lying and half-truths, a further and radical turning toward the One who is the way, truth, and life (John 14:6).

2

The Lie of Express Conversion

How the Savior Saves Us

> The coming of the lawless one is apparent in the working of Satan, who uses all power, signs, lying wonders, and every kind of wicked deception for those who are perishing, because they refused to love the truth and so be saved. . . . But we must always give thanks to God for you, brothers and sisters beloved by the Lord, because God chose you as the first fruits for salvation through sanctification by the Spirit and through belief in the truth.
>
> 2 Thessalonians 2:9–10, 13

> Remember the long way that the LORD your God has led you these forty years in the wilderness.
>
> Deuteronomy 8:2

Even if I'm only partially correct about the church's general inattention to "the devil and all his empty promises," I suspect that Satan (or whatever you'd like to call him/her) appreciates the resulting ability to fly under the radar. Flamboyant lies and sins grab our attention in various media, while more subtle half-truths and deceits get winked at and largely ignored in parish life. This is why any church worth its salt (see Matt. 5:13 and Col. 4:6) will acknowledge that true conversion takes time. Detoxification from the surrounding culture is a lifelong endeavor prompted and sustained by the Holy Spirit.

A specific *process* of adult conversion must be in place in congregational life—something much more than six weeks of instruction and a handshake into church membership. Otherwise we are fooling ourselves into believing that the kind of discipleship Jesus had in mind is actually occurring. Most pastors know that "the life and witness of the church faces many challenges in a pluralistic society like our own. . . . One challenge further complicates the situation for the church; a challenge to be faced within its own walls. This challenge is the problem of nominal membership. For many people, church membership and Christian commitment have become peripheral rather than central to their lives."[1] The problem of so-called "back door losses" (losing people soon after they join up) can be directly related to the fact that new members sense that absolutely nothing is expected or at stake when they sign on with Jesus.

I go back and forth about whether a conversion process should be required of new converts who join our congregation (or whether church council members should be required to pass a basic inventory on Bible knowledge before becoming a leader). The brevity of instruction[2] and quick baptismal plunging of the Ethiopian eunuch (Acts 8:36) always gives me pause about ecclesiastical legislation in this regard. But I'm convinced that such a process should be in place and *strongly encouraged* for anyone seeking adult baptism or returning to

21

parish life after a long absence. In fifteen years of offering a conversion process (outlined later in this chapter) in two parishes, no one has charged that this might create some sort of us-versus-them tension between those who seek discipleship depth and those who don't. That tension is probably present on some level before anything of formal depth is offered.

The temptation to offer the faithful a shortcut is old (read the very juicy twenty-eighth chapter of Jeremiah before proceeding). Hananiah preached the express exile, a popular sermon compared to Jeremiah's honest admission that life in exile would take much longer. People wanted to believe Hananiah, but he was wrong. Jeremiah dared to tell the truth that day. In an era of instant gratification, it is tempting for churches to offer new members a quick and easy express entrance into church membership, as accessible and trouble-free as possible. New members often do not like hearing that listening and waiting for God's Word may take some time. But shortcuts into the body of Christ are not delineated in either testament.

Trust me. There will always be a church in your neighborhood offering glitzy programming and shortcuts to knowing Jesus. There may *not* be a congregation in your town actually offering a process of conversion that truly matters. Become known for helping parishioners through the lengthier, truer process. I offer two words of advice for pastors who may encounter church-shoppers who threaten to locate a more palatable way to Jesus and depart for another option just down the street: *let them*. The paradoxical truth of Jesus takes time to convey and time to sink in,[3] which is a challenge for all of us living in the age of information. Garret Keizer says this well using an analogy from adolescence; here he describes an eight-year-old boy who discovers a skin magazine and then concludes that he knows all about women:

Because here is a picture of one, all bare and in living color, and here are some very important facts about her: Tiffany likes windsurfing, a good Chablis, and the sort of man who knows how to take charge. But the little boy doesn't know about women. He doesn't even know about Tiffany. Knowledge of that sort can only come in relationship. You don't Google a person or a faith tradition. You live with it. You keep faith with it, and sometimes you break up with it. No picnic either way.[4]

Jesus and his community cannot be grasped in small informational doses but only through unhurried, percolated time. "By not seeing that we Christians are a tribe, we lose sight of the fact that becoming a member of that tribe is a lifelong process—as it would be with any other tribe. It's not accomplished over a weekend. It involves study, acculturation, and learning new habits."[5] In the pages that follow, I will describe our local process of conversion in some detail. But let me explain more fully why such a process is needed in the first place.

Church of Scars

I've met very few people who say that high school was a swell and fun time. Our bodies behave in strange ways hormonally. We do and say cruel things to one another without thinking through the ramifications of our actions and words. And dating is rather awkward. At least it was for me.

I went on only two real dates in high school, one of which was with a stunning girl who was completely out of my league. Somehow I summoned the nerve to ask her to a movie. I think she said *yes* out of sympathy and kindness. She was very sweet. I had other things besides sweetness on my mind, despite the fact that I was a world-class dork.

We went to see the movie *Jaws*—that summer blockbuster from the mid '70s that brought sharks as big as houses into

23

the national imagination. I also recall fantasizing that perhaps my date would need to depend on a masculine shoulder in the face of such marine carnage. The truth of the matter is that my hands never stopped gripping my own armrests throughout the movie. She may not have been safe at the shore that summer, but by golly she was certainly safe from me that night.

One of the few funny scenes in the movie takes place when Richard Dreyfuss and his companions start comparing mishaps—boating accidents, shark and barracuda bites—around the table one night. They are rather drunk and begin showing each other their scars. A shirt is pulled up. A sock is tugged off. Pants are pulled down. These old sailors, utterly engaged in the art of one-upmanship, reveal more and more of their gouged flesh—their old, dated scars. More and more clothing falls to the floor until they're standing in little more than their underwear. They finally look at each other, throw back their heads, and laugh. I think the shark bumps the boat right after that.

Jesus reveals himself to the disciples several times after his crucifixion, but my favorite episode is found in John 20:19–29. The disciples are together on that first Easter evening, cowering behind locked doors in fear. And who can blame them? Crucifixions in those parts were contagious. Mary has reported the fantastic, far-fetched events of the morning. Suddenly Jesus stands among them and says, "Peace be with you." But they don't put two and two together. Not just yet. I don't know what they thought they were looking at, but they weren't thinking Jesus.

Then Jesus lifted up his shirt and pointed to the scar on his side. Then he pulled back the sleeves on his robe and showed them his palms. Maybe he even pulled off his sandals and showed them his feet. At any rate, he revealed how the

Romans had roughed him up. The text reports these words in verse 20: "Then the disciples rejoiced when they saw the Lord." *Then.* Not a moment sooner. Here's an important detail for latter-day followers. Those early disciples did not have a clue about who was standing before them until Jesus showed them his scars. Only then did they rejoice.

Near the end of Homer's epic, *The Odyssey*, Odysseus finally returns home after all his years of travel. But when he comes home he's disguised as an old man. The aging family nurse, Eurycleia, begins to bathe the man whom she thinks is nobody more than some old stranger. Only when she sees Odysseus's old hunting wound, inflicted by a boar in his youth, does she come to recognition. Listen to these words from Homer: "This was the scar the old nurse recognized; she traced it under her spread hands, then let it go, and into the basin fell the lower leg . . . sloshing the water out. Her eyes filled up with tears; her throat closed and she whispered . . . '*You are Odysseus!* Ah dear child! I could not see you until now.' "[6]

Jesus showed them his wounds. The disciples rejoiced when they saw Jesus. They could not see him until then. Here we have a risen Jesus, safe and sound in the bosom of his Father, past the trauma of Good Friday, nothin' but good times ahead, and his friends don't really have a clue who he is until he shows them his scars. There's a profound connection between the risen Christ and the scars of Christ. Easter does not totally negate Good Friday.

"Jesus will always bring you peace and joy." Ever heard anyone say that? "If you're a *real* Christian, you'll always have peace in your heart." Well, what if you feel great sadness? Does that mean you're *not* a real Christian? People bear real and traumatic scars from a real and traumatic past. But when Jesus comes into our lives, we are sometimes led to believe that everything will be rosy. Not only do I think

25

that's hogwash, but I'm also pretty certain that *Jesus* thinks it's hogwash.

"He showed them his hands and his side." It wasn't a heavenly cloud that brought those Easter disciples a sense of peace and recognition. It was a scarred Jesus who dared to show them his wounds. Even Easter does not erase scars.

So what does this story say about the modern church? What does it say about all of us who carry around scars and old wounds? It means that we are to find a way to show *our scars* to one another. To stop pretending they don't exist and stop believing the lie that good Christians (with the right sort of faith) don't have such scars. How will we show one another our old wounds and our present scars?

We've been sharing the peace in the Lutheran liturgy since at least 1978, when the old green *Lutheran Book of Worship* made its debut. The practice actually goes back to biblical times, but perhaps nothing has generated more controversy and resistance in liturgical reform among many Lutherans than this ancient and very scriptural action in our worship order just before the celebration of Holy Communion.

I've often wondered what would happen if Christians took our cues from Jesus in sharing the peace. "Peace be with you, Madge, and now take a gander at my cardiac bypass incision." "Peace be with you, Randy, and now let me tell you about my bills I had a hard time paying last month." "Peace of the Lord be with you, Sally, and I'm sure you've heard by now about my nephew who's struggling with a drug problem."[7]

Perhaps this is what the doubting Thomases outside (and inside) church life are really looking for. *Authenticity*. Do such people doubt Jesus? Or do they doubt his body, the church? Church is not about starched people who assemble for an hour each week, knowing very little about one another. Church is about gathering around a *scarred Lord* who profoundly touches our *own scars* and unites us in community with precisely what we have in common—not our potential, not our social standing, not even our denominational theology, but mainly our wounds and how the gospel prepares us to enter into and share the wounds of others. If we're not about that, we're not about the gospel.

"Unless I see the mark of the nails in his hands, I will not believe," said Thomas.

Jesus bore scars even on Easter. So must we come to terms with our own. Our scars are a large part of who we are. As we share them in community, perhaps Christ is saying, "Ah, dear children. I could not fully see you. I could not see you until now."

Genealogy: Doxology and Lament

As you've no doubt observed, God creates some very interesting people. His fallen creation, however, leaves us wounded and scarred, complicated and warped even further by the Father of Lies. Ours are very old stories with generational patterns of dysfunction. There is hope, however. God has given us very old stories as solutions. If conversion is authentic, we need to understand clearly the cards we've been dealt and what makes us all tick. Here's an old family story full of old scars—mine. I'll come back to the even older stories God provides for the healing of any human family. Given the fall and human pride and all the other seven deadly sins, this is what God has to work with—both in my own family and in all the interesting characters of the book we call the Bible.

• • •

I was born on May 15, 1957, in Chattanooga, Tennessee, the middle son of Ruth and Bob Honeycutt's three boys. I'm named for my great-grandfather Frank,[8] who was sheriff of Cabarrus County, North Carolina, from 1908 to1914. On December 18, 1908,[9] Sheriff Frank presided over the last legal public hanging in the state, even though he was personally opposed to capital punishment. The prisoner executed that day was an African American man accused of raping a white woman.[10] The man was later found to be innocent.

I cannot remember my baptism, though it did occur on July 28, 1957, at Ascension Lutheran (downtown—now torn down) at the hands of the Lord and Pastor Jim Cadwallader. I'd never laid anything but baby eyes on Jim until 1985, when his name appeared on our congregational prayer list where I was serving in Stephens City, Virginia. The name clicked as my child baptizer. We met on July 28 that year and had a baptism party with our family and his. He died a month later.

Life with my family on Chattanooga's Elaine Trail was always interesting. Our house was basically peaceful and supportive. Like most young boys, I fought with my brothers, once seriously injured my little brother, Lee, by kicking him in the groin. My mother, an inner-city reading specialist, told me, "Don't you *ever* kick someone there unless you're defending yourself against an actual enemy." My older brother, Mike, knocked me out cold once at age seven outside Cawood's Barber Shop. I don't remember why. The barber was aghast. Mike is an electronic and mechanical genius who is now a retired engineer living just outside Asheville. He wrote love letters to North Carolina's Jesse Helms until Jesse's recent death. Lee teaches at Iowa State University, in the English department. He worked for the George McGovern campaign at age fourteen and campaigned in 2008 for Barack Obama. My dad votes Republican almost every time. We had interesting dinner conversations growing up—still do when we all gather at the beach each summer.

Growing up we all dutifully went to church and prayed at meals—all the cozy Protestant habits. My parents tired of Pastor Brewer's overt political leanings from the pulpit (this was the Vietnam era), and we moved across town to Trinity. I was very unhappy about this move and was never very active at our new church, probably in an attempt to punish my parents.

Girls were a mystery to me. I was very shy around them and didn't actually kiss one until my senior year in high school. But backing up: I don't remember any really traumatic events. My fifth-grade teacher, Mildred Chaffin (a devout Baptist who preached in class), had me believing the inevitability of divorce for all couples who even raised their voices to one another, or who were outside the Lord. We were inside the Lord (I perceived), but a fifth grader is prone to fantasy. My parents actually have a wonderful marriage (fifty-four years) and provided a safe home where thinking and difference of opinion were not only tolerated but also encouraged. But our conversations had an edge sometimes.

I've saved a cartoon from the *New Yorker* for several years now.[11] A father sits in a lounger and speaks caringly (but rather judgmentally) to his two children. The father is bundled in several layers of clothing, a scarf, and a warm cap. The children are standing beside him, shivering. You can see their frosty breath hang in the air. It's cold in the house. The caption reads: "With the cost of heating oil at an all-time high, perhaps you now regret exchanging those sensible Christmas sweaters for the fleeting amusement of toys." That father is me—funny but sometimes smug and acerbic. I get it honestly.

My mother's side of the family has struggled for many generations (in fits and starts) with depression. When my mom's dad died in the summer of 1973, she was prowling

29

around her parents' attic in Brevard, North Carolina, and kept coming across the name "Eulie." After a thorough search, mom discovered that her mother's sister had been whisked away from the family to a sanitarium just east of Memphis, diagnosed with what was probably schizophrenia, and never spoken of in the family again. My mother, one of the most determined and courageous women I've ever known, made a trip soon thereafter to visit her Aunt Eulie for the very first time.

As I said, we all gather at a beach house every summer in North Carolina and have a great time catching up and telling stories. But after a point, I retreat alone to the upper deck of the house. People think I want to read quietly. No—sometimes I'm running away from us, and from me.

In 1971 I was plucked out of the public school system (an irony to me given my mother's vocation) and swept away to a private school called the McCallie School. I was transferred mostly out of fear, some of which may have been justifiable. Race riots, stabbings, threats, and other kinds of violence were commonplace in the high schools. The environment of intimidation made it hard for my older brother even to walk to class or use the school's bathroom. We were white and we took flight. Don't get me wrong—the all-male school we transferred to was an exceptional place. I took courses in Twain and Shakespeare and was able to study advanced calculus in the eleventh grade.

In a word, though, I hated the McCallie School until my senior year, when I made a few lasting friendships. It was a protected, privileged, sheltered place. Having left the church after my ninth-grade confirmation, though, it was one of my senior-year friends ("Moon Goon," a.k.a. Doug Sullivan— now a Princeton Seminary grad and Ole Miss professor) who got me thinking about church again.

After graduation, I went to Clemson, three states away in South Carolina. No one I knew went there. I was on my own and scared. In the first week I thought about going home and somehow wandered into the office of Gene Copenhaver, the Lutheran campus minister. He immediately understood the alienation I was struggling with. He invited me to go out to the lake and check on his sailboat. He also asked a Lutheran upperclassman to check on me regularly. My new connection led to an intense involvement in the campus church and a subsequent interest in seminary. God's odd sense of humor and influence of Gene and Pastor Ron Luckey are no doubt the two main reasons I'm a pastor.

College was incredibly fun for me. I goofed off, was never really challenged academically, and coasted through with As and Bs. It was a happy time with many close friendships. I did almost kill myself twice in encounters with a dam (I dove off, stupidly) and a drugged-out gunman in downtown Charleston at 2:00 a.m.—don't ask me what I was doing there.

I spent my collegiate summers at summer camp. I met my wife, Cindy, at Camp Lutheridge near Asheville. Cindy is perhaps the most compassionate person I've ever met, and I wake up most mornings feeling quite unworthy to be her husband. I met my good friend, and committed atheist, Andy, at Camp Hope near Clemson, where we worked with disabled children and adults. Andy now lives alone in the Maine wilderness on fifty acres with no electricity or indoor plumbing. In very different ways Cindy and Andy taught me about God and were the two most important shapers of my life after college. I walked three hundred miles of the Appalachian Trail with Andy, five hundred with Cindy, and the rest of the thirteen hundred miles alone. There is hardly a day that goes by that I don't think about the trail.

For a year after college I taught school in Camden with a group of twelve educable mentally handicapped students. It was wild. They were wild. My landlady in Camden threatened to kick me out of Kirkwood apartment 3B due to a racially integrated cookout I had for my class during the spring. I told her off. She backed down. She too is a child of God.

After the Appalachian Trail hike, I entered seminary kicking and screaming. I wasn't sure whether I'd last a year. But I loved it and asked every question I could conjure. Professors were patient with me, and I developed a reputation as something of a rebel. Stephens City, Virginia, was our first call. Hannah was born one week after our arrival. I served two churches there—one tiny church in apple country and a town church that grew until they needed their own pastor. We moved to Abingdon, the other end of Virginia.

I had a brief brush with testicular cancer in 1998, a period that included surgery and radiation treatments. I'm fine these days, but that hospitalization and illness taught me a lot about what it was like to be on the other side of a hospital bed. Of course, as a pastor I'm in and out of hospitals a lot.

Cindy and I have been married for twenty-eight years. We're almost polar opposites in personality. God brought us together for a reason, but I'm not sure anyone could have easily predicted that reason. We've had our share of misunderstandings. My daughter Hannah, now twenty-four, is our only biological child. I once jokingly complained to Hannah that Hallmark had never come up with a greeting card for Good Friday. As a young teenager, she created her own set of cards with black construction paper, bound them with a pink ribbon, and presented them to me on that famous Friday. The inside of each card read: *May All Your Dreams Come True on This Dark Day of Our Lord's Death.* Marta, now twenty-two, came to us from El Salvador when she was eleven months old. We could afford only one plane ticket, so Cindy whisked her home while the Salvadoran war raged all around the capital. The orphanage where Marta spent her first days was destroyed by an earthquake. Marta is our most outgoing child—she has more friends than I have by far. Lukas, now eighteen, is biracial. He has an African American birth father and Caucasian birth mother. Lukas's birth mother lived in a small Tennessee town where such births were not warmly welcomed by the locals. Lukas is wickedly and darkly funny. We've had volcanic arguments,[12] but always seem to make up and laugh a lot together. I don't believe we were brought together by accident. Some days we are an argument waiting to happen, but mostly we love each other well. We're learning to speak the truth along with that love.

Our family was birthed by God in baptism. We are a theological lab of sorts for working out the issues raised in the last chapter and the challenges surrounding authentic Christian conversion. I didn't realize how true this is until very recently.

Today, almost seven years into a call at Ebenezer, I'm finally scratching the surface of what it means to be a pastor for this parish. I feel more called to my vocation than ever before. It's an odd life. Every day I begin again. I once had a visit from a woman who refused to join a church because it was filled with hypocrites. I am indeed one. The truth lies somewhere amid embracing our common hypocrisy and allowing Jesus to lead us to a new place, sometimes against our will or common sense.

• • •

I'm holding a very old picture showing a baptism in Helton Creek, Virginia, near where I used to serve as pastor for fourteen years. The date is 1922. The local Methodist congregation under the leadership of Pastor Blankenship stands in and all around the water. My friend's aunt Bessie (then a very young woman) is about to be baptized. The women wear bonnets. The men wear hats. One child on the opposite bank watches the scene in utter astonishment and awe. Her mouth is open. A woman on dry land wipes away sweat (or maybe a tear). Pastor Blankenship has his eyes closed, head toward heaven, right arm raised in blessing. Bessie looks down at the water. She looks sad, as if someone has just died and she's leaving something behind. She's about to enter the creek, go under, and rise to another life.

Conversion: Theology and Practice

> If any doctrines within the whole compass of Christianity may be properly termed fundamental, they are doubtless these two—the doctrine of justification, and that of the new birth: The former relating to that great work which God does *for us*, in forgiving our sins; the latter to the great work which God does *in us*, in renewing our fallen nature.[13]
>
> John Wesley

In the summer of 1982, I did my Clinical Pastoral Education (CPE) in a prison setting, the Central Correctional Institution (CCI) on the banks of the Congaree River, which flows through the city of Columbia. The old dungeonlike facility is now torn down, and an upscale housing development is emerging in its place.

At CCI, I met a guy named Pee Wee Gaskins. Great guy on the surface; also a notorious serial killer. Pee Wee asked for communion just before I left the prison that summer to return to seminary. A couple of months later he was linked to (and eventually executed for) a strange in-house radio bomb that killed a fellow inmate. I've often wondered whether Pee Wee asked for communion as some sort of pre-crime absolution for what he was hatching. Sometimes Christians think conversion is only for flamboyant and notorious sinners like Pee Wee.

Conversion is always a lifelong process—never finished for any of us. "For while we are still in this tent, we groan under our burden, because we wish not to be unclothed but to be further clothed, so that what is mortal may be swallowed up in life" (2 Cor. 5:4). Six weeks of instruction in an inquirers' class and a handshake into church membership isn't going to foil the Father of Lies. It never has. "The number of people who claim to have been Christians for years but who lack spiritual depth and maturity is reason for alarm," writes Gordon T. Smith. "Consider the possibility that at least part of the root of this problem is a weak understanding of Christian conversion."[14]

In his excellent book, *Beginning Well*, Smith suggests that renewal will not occur in churches until pastors and parishioners embrace three specific things:[15] (1) a "clear goal" that moves the justified sinner from acceptance and forgiveness in Christ to growth in holiness (sanctification); (2) a "good beginning" in which a local congregation expects and looks out for people who are turning to Jesus, assisting new converts in this turning and helping them become conversant in the vocabulary of conversion; and (3) an "intentional program of spiritual formation" in which newcomers are invited to grow in faith alongside other converts and seasoned church members. "Many Christians," says Smith, "have anemic spiritual lives with little freedom, little growth in grace and little commitment to obedience and service. I propose that an appropriate response to this predicament includes facing up to the fact that the church has a weak notion of conversion."[16]

I don't know about your denomination, but this describes the current Lutheran predicament in spades. In the name of grace, we justify just about any behavior or lack of spiritual discipline. Many Lutheran clergy, seeking to avoid the horrid sin of seeming judgmental, slowly begin to resemble Pastor Misty Naylor in Garrison Keillor's novel *Pontoon*: "She used to be Presbyterian but she had a near-death experience during breast enhancement surgery and a door opened onto a garden full of golden light and beautiful plants and every different sort of person, Muslim and Hindu and Buddhist and Jew, all rejoicing and living in harmony, and when Misty returned to life, she dedicated herself to world peace and to Momentism—you know, the idea that all of time takes place in one moment, there is no eternity."[17]

Bending over backward to avoid judgment in the name of grace, Lutherans sometimes fall into the world's great religious salad bar and form "theology amalgamated"—a little of this, a little of that, and nothing really in particular. Because they want to avoid legalism, it's hard for many Lutherans to get theologically specific anymore: "For we ourselves were once foolish, disobedient, led astray, slaves to various passions and pleasures, passing our days in malice and envy, despicable, hating one another. But when the goodness and loving kindness of God our Savior appeared, he saved us, not because of any works of righteousness that we had done, but according to his mercy, through the water of rebirth and renewal by the Holy Spirit" (Titus 3:3–5).

● ● ●

I can see it in their eyes. It's orientation night for those who are considering our Ebenezer catechumenal process.

You want me to do all that? Five people eventually sign on for the eight-month process. Those who don't have the time or inclination are invited back the following year, and I encourage them to experience the many short-term opportunities we have at Ebenezer on Sunday mornings and throughout the week. On a Monday evening at 7:45 p.m., the five recruits gather with me in my office for the first of our weekly ninety-minute meetings that will occur over the church year. We're such a varied bunch, and as the catechist I always wonder at this point whether we'll ever gel and make it through the first month. It's also apparent that we bring our histories and hurts with us. James reminds the early church, "Whenever you face trials of any kind, consider it nothing but joy, because you know that the testing of your faith produces endurance; and let endurance have its full effect, so that you may be mature and complete, lacking in nothing" (James 1:2–4). From the first meeting, it's clear that we've all endured a lot. I'm not sure that the group, however, "considers it all joy" at this point. Let's look at them one by one.

Emerson[18] grew up in a strict religious tradition that required a nightly recitation of each and every sin for that day. He left the church after discovering that what he'd been taught did not square with the true facts of the church's origins. "I was so angry that I'd been bamboozled, and I was determined to never, ever be fooled again when it comes to religious belief." After getting married and having children of his own, Emerson recently found his way back to church but admits that "distrust of religious authority sometimes gets in the way."

Cleo, daughter of a retired pastor, is a lesbian and a long-time Christian. "About seventh grade, I started to resent the church because, despite our differences and his propensity for angry discipline, I really missed my father. He worked all the time. The church had stolen my daddy." Cleo is recovering from a recent breakup with her longtime partner and is seeking new employment as this process begins.

Mary, a health professional, tentatively plans to be baptized at the Easter Vigil but wants to take time to learn more. She grew up with no church tradition at all. "I can remember my friends asking me what religion I was and being mortified that we were 'nothing.' When I asked my parents why we didn't go to church, my mom would blame it on the fact that we moved around so much, and at the time that seemed like a good answer. I remember our first cross-country meet when our coach led us in the Lord's Prayer before the race. Thank goodness that people look down when they pray because I knew only a few of the words."

Race manages his own business and has been a member of our congregation for about ten years. "As long as I can remember I have sensed the presence of God. Often times at church I felt this presence. But I have felt most spiritual in nature. At an early age I became amazed with plants. I actually did not mind doing yard work and gardening." Race seeks a deeper discipleship through this group.

Sally has taught special education in public schools for many years; she's been a Lutheran since her marriage. "During my worst depressions I had one friend who called me often and would not let me push her away. She showed me a theology of love and never used dogma or absolutes." Naturally inquisitive and skeptical, Sally comes to group life with "lots of questions" about God and the Bible. She is particularly interested in learning more about how to share her faith with others without sounding judgmental.

After an opening prayer on a chilly October evening, we begin.

• • •

The Catechumenal Process

> You go out into deep waters to save, and you do so because
> you love. But the assumption that you are perched above the
> water and that the person you're addressing is drowning pre-
> vents real empathy. You will never understand that person's
> mystery until you abandon the need to move her where you
> are, to leave her where you yourself don't want to be. Because
> every evangelical knows, in the end, that the act of conversion
> is a mystery.[19]
>
> Todd Shy

The catechumenal process hearkens back to the early centuries of the church. Partly acknowledging the difficulty in
converting from a pagan culture to a Christian community,
and partly recognizing the need (from fear of infiltration and
exposure to Roman oppression) to look over converts closely
before welcoming them fully, conversion to Jesus in the first
few centuries of the church was usually a long and protracted
process lasting up to three years. It culminated with baptism
at the Great Easter Vigil. The conversion of Constantine in the
early fourth century generally lessened the rigors a catechu-
men might face in preparing for baptism. (In many Lutheran
settings, a theology of infant baptism often calls into question
any preparation at all for parents or adult converts.) Used by
missionaries for many years (particularly those in Africa), the
catechumenal process was recovered in the United States in
the 1960s when Roman Catholics began using RCIA, "The
Rite of Christian Initiation for Adults." Liturgical traditions
(particularly Lutherans and Episcopalians) soon followed
suit with their own rites and local processes.

Many books[20] describe what some call "liturgical evangelism." Local processes differ from place to place. Some include

only true catechumens (adults preparing for baptism), and others also include people who have been away from church life for some time and are now returning as adults.[21] Whatever the local practice, the catechumenate generally includes four stages that lead participants to conclude, "He has rescued us from the power of darkness and transferred us into the kingdom of his beloved Son" (Col. 1:13), and "It is no longer I who live, but it is Christ who lives in me" (Gal. 2:20). Here's how the catechumenal process has worked in the two settings I've served in—one small town and one urban inner city—since 1994. In fifteen years of trial and error, about seventy-five people have gone through the process under my, or a lay catechist's, leadership. That may not seem like a lot, but one must remember that these seventy-five have a clear sense of their call over unhurried, percolated time. Alternately, many of the new member class (the six-week course that surely has a place in church life) graduates who have "joined" the church subsequently vanish.

The four stages I will briefly describe here go by different names, but most expressions of the catechumenal process roughly coincide with the powerful cyclical nature of the church year. The paragraphs that follow are a very brief tour through these stages, with the theme of this book in mind.

Stage 1 begins with a signed agreement to meet at a particular time and place on a weekly basis. Confidentiality is stressed and revisited many times. All members of the group receive a copy of what we've agreed upon. A built-in exit possibility is included at the end of the first stage. I'll note here that one young man in a group I led was three months into the process before finally deciding that he did not want to be baptized. It was an agonizing part of group life that year to pray with Alex and say good-bye. He continued to worship with us for a while and then disappeared entirely. This is an important part of any conversion process seeking to speak the truth in love: there can be no coercion or arm-twisting. A disciple of Jesus must feel called and not pushed. "If any *want* to become my followers, let them deny themselves and take up their cross and follow me" (Mark 8:34). Part of the challenge of member inactivity in our congregations is that we do not engage new people on this very point—call and commitment. Commitment will not seem like a burden if the call is authentic.

The curriculum for this first stage consists of the questions brought by the members of the group. *Who created God? Why is there so much suffering in the world if God is good? How do I read the Bible and take even the strange stories seriously? Why should I be a Christian and not a Buddhist? What do Christians believe about hell and heaven?* One goal of the inquiry stage is to honor the truth that God has been at work in the lives of participants well before their entrance into congregational life. So it's important to honor their questions as signs of the living God at work before church became a consideration. All questions are arranged by topic, typed, and distributed to group members early in this first stage. It is very important to take seriously all questions. One of the catechist's primary requirements early on is transparency. No question is out of bounds. I always like to recall that the first words out of Jesus's mouth in the Gospel of John come in the form of a question: "What are you looking for?" (1:38). Reading assignments (short articles dealing with specific questions) may be part of this first stage, but conversation, testimony, and honest exchange color most of our time together between early October and the beginning of Advent.

Inquiry, of course, never really ends for any of us. But toward the end of this first stage, participants engage in a weeklong period of discernment to decide whether they want to move on to the next stage. By this time, most decide to continue. Others who may not have the time or theological inclination are blessed by the group without judgment. Church staff should always follow up with those who decide not to continue and invite them into other areas of involvement in church life. Those who choose to continue mark this decision with a public rite at one of the Sunday morning services. The central question posed in that rite is the same question posed by Jesus in John 1:38: "What are you looking for?" or "What do you seek?" Participants may answer, "Life in Christ," or they may answer with words of their own.

Stage 2 roughly coincides with the period from the beginning of Advent through the end of Epiphany. And here the group wrestles collectively (and individually) with important questions shaped by the church year: *What am I pregnant with; what is waiting to be born? What gifts (with the magi) might I be able to offer Jesus?*

This stage of the process is characterized by two central things, which take up the lion's share of time between early December and Lent—spiritual autobiographies and Bible study on one of the lectionary lessons for the coming Sunday. All five of the participants named above chose to continue in the process. I (or the lay catechist) always go first in sharing an autobiography that describes God's presence (or seeming absence) in childhood, adolescence, young adulthood, and current experience.[22] At this point, confidentiality must be stressed once again. Many are revisiting old wounds in their writing for the first time in years. It is especially important to remind the group that we are not serving in a therapeutic fashion but rather as colleagues on a theological quest for meaning and truth.

Bible study in this stage is characterized by the simple (but profound) method of *lectio divina*—a slow rereading of one of the lectionary texts for the coming Sunday. This serves as excellent preparation for worship and helps participants begin to see their stories in the overarching metanarrative that is the Bible. Stage 2 concludes with another public rite. The result is that other parishioners continue to become aware of the group's existence for prayerful support and possible participation in a future year.

Stage 3 coincides with Lent and all the services of Holy Week. The central questions of this stage are: *What is dying within me to make room for something else? What am I leaving behind?* We talk candidly about and experiment with the central Lenten disciplines of prayer, fasting, almsgiving, and service in the community. Weekly Bible study on the lectionary texts continues. As a preacher, I've noticed that group participants are helping me formulate the sermon by this point in our lives together. Holy Week is an especially rich and meaningful time. We all prepare for Mary's baptism (with her young daughter) at the Easter Vigil with anticipation and joy. Cleo twitters that the idea of washing feet on Maundy Thursday at the noon service gives her "the heebie-jeebies." I try to explain some of the drama of the Triduum, but not too much. Stripping an altar as the shadows lengthen, the reading of John's passion narrative on that famous Friday, and the mystery of fire, water, and Word at the Vigil all carry powerful unspoken metaphors that cannot be described fully beforehand. Experiencing the fullness of Lent and Holy Week together is always powerful and moving: "Now that you have purified your souls by your obedience to the truth so that you have genuine mutual love, love one another deeply from the heart. You have been born anew, not of perishable but of imperishable seed, through the living and enduring word of God" (1 Pet. 1:22–23).

Stage 4 (coinciding with the fifty days of Easter) is also called mystagogy in many catechumenal process variations.

During this stage, we reflect on the sacramental mysteries of Holy Communion and baptism. At Ebenezer Church we also use a gift-discernment process and focus on a final question: *How is Christ alive inside me after I have died with him in baptism?* "For you have died, and your life is hidden with Christ in God" (Col. 3:3).

By this time, after months of weekly meetings, the group knows one another quite well and can take some risks, stating the unique spiritual gifts that each participant brings to the body. Race has a gift and love for yard work and plans to use his time sacrificially to beautify the church grounds. Mary senses her gift (as a newly baptized person) in the ministry of accompaniment for other unbaptized adults who are joining us for worship on Sundays. We all sense a great need for retreat ministry at Ebenezer, and Sally shares her history of experiencing the Spirit's power in settings away from an urban pace. She expresses a desire to start a regular retreat ministry in our congregation. Emerson thinks hard theologically, and we all agree that he's being called by God to teach adults and maybe serve as a lay catechist in this process. Cleo feels a tug to reach out in Christ's name to other gay and lesbian people who feel estranged from Christ's church. On the day of Pentecost, the group stands before the congregation and announces a specific call into ministry. Others in the congregation are invited to gather around this call and begin a new (or support an existing) ministry. The Holy Spirit descends anew. Scales fall from our eyes. The church is renewed and strengthened through the gift of call and conversion.

Loving As Jesus Loved

We reveal what we think Christian witness is all about with the standards and practices we establish for becoming a Christian. If we accept a "lowest common denominator" definition of

Christian commitment, then we should not be surprised that our congregations evidence so little commitment to gospel mission.[23]

Darrell L. Guder

The Bible is a difficult book to believe. Stars speak (Bar. 3:34). Donkeys confront the wayward (Num. 22:28). She-bears maul sassy children (2 Kings 2:24). Narcoleptic parishioners fall to their death out of windows during sermons (Acts 20:9). Karl Barth was correct and prescient for a new generation of global seekers when he wrote about the "strange new world within the Bible."[24] My work with catechumens new to church life reveals that many people are thirsty for a story that makes sense of their own personal stories. The pages of the Bible are no less (or more) weird than what many are experiencing in daily life—might as well go with the God revealed to the prophet Ezekiel, who writes, "Like the bow in a cloud on a rainy day, such was the appearance of the splendor all around. This was the appearance of the likeness of the glory of the Lord" (Ezek. 1:28).

Darrel Guder (quoted above) calls pastors to an exciting task: "Our congregations today urgently need to be ministered to by evangelist-pastors. That does not mean that they should hear a sermon every Sunday about accepting Christ. They should hear, instead, the constant and empowered message of good news which calls all Christians to continuing conversion, to growth and healing in the life of faith, and to greater and more radical obedience as sent-out witnesses."[25] Taking my cue from Guder (and serving as a segue to the second section of this book), I offer the following reflection from Jesus as he prepares to leave his followers for a while and sends them out into an uncertain world.

● ● ●

It's not considered one of his famous "last seven," but of all the words that Jesus shared with his disciples during the week we call holy, a tiny two-letter word ought to send shivers down the spine of the church. "Just as I have loved you, you also should love one another" (John 13:34). I really wish Jesus hadn't said that. I'd prefer a suggestion (not a commandment) that our love might occasionally, on our best days, attempt to *resemble* his. Now wouldn't that be enough? I would also be happy with the word *approximate*. Heck, I'd settle for "just try to come close from time to time." "In the same ballpark" would be comforting. But he didn't use any of those phrases. He used the tiniest of words: *as*. "Love *as* I have loved."

And if we really hear that little word, maybe really hear it for the first time, I wouldn't blame anyone if they bolted for the church door and never looked back. Because if I'm hearing Jesus correctly, it means the cross is not just a dusty old event we recall and dramatically reenact each year, a religious relic for which we're very grateful.

Curiously, the cross is not just the way Jesus loved us, it's also the way we love *each other*. Our love takes a cruciform shape, sacrificing personal needs and wants for the sake of others. On one level, we might truly begin to fathom the gracious power of a man offering his life for our sin. That's one thing. But when he says, "Love this way, just *as* I have loved you," no one would blame you for rethinking this church business. As Daniel Berrigan, a Jesuit priest, once put it, "A Christian should be prepared to look good on wood."[26]

But a question is in order. And this is for all who choose not to run from this little adverb. Jesus may have said to love this way, but how in the world do we do it? How do we teach such love in the church? And to our children? A recent cover story in *Newsweek* magazine reported that we are now liv-

46

ing in post-Christian America. Never before has the teaching ministry of the church been more important in our country as we describe to people (perhaps for their first hearing) what a Christian disciple actually is and how a person becomes one. So how do we live sacrificially and for others? How do our lives begin to take the shape of a cross? How do we actually embody this little two-letter word, loving *as* Jesus loved?

Well, some have tried through personal willpower. Do we simply decide one Sunday morning that from now on, by golly, we're going to try our darnedest to live this way? Or do we perhaps try and scold people into loving as Jesus did? Tell them things like, "You *oughta* love like Jesus loved after all he's done for you, you ungrateful little wretch." A lot of Christian preaching (including my own, I fear) must sound a lot like that.

One of the things I find somewhat simplistic about the "What Would Jesus Do?" movement is that presumably one is to discover WWJD and then just do that very thing. Just get out there and do it. I recall those Michael Jordan TV commercials in which young adolescents were invited to "just do it." Just get in there and be Michael, forgetting the years of practice and toil it took to become such a great basketball player. It's like telling a young person to sit down at a piano keyboard for the first time and just go ahead and play Chopin before they've taken time to learn the scales. I'm unconvinced that individual willpower or manipulative scolding will teach children or adults very much about loving as Jesus loved. So what will?

The old story (John 13:1–35) framing Jesus's commandment is full of details that tell us about God and life with God—details about loving as Jesus loved. How he did it and how we might. Three specific things surface from these verses.

First, I'm struck in chapter 13 of John with this amazing claim: Jesus knew that "he had come from God, and was going to God" (v. 3). Think hard about those words. Jesus had such a clear awareness of his origins. *And* he knew that he was returning to those origins. A modern way of saying this is that his identity was utterly intact. When it really hits us that we are loved by God, that in baptism we are born of God and that we will return to God, then there is really not a thing in this life that can trump that, nothing that can jump out and get us, because *God's already got us.*

Now that might seem like a rather ludicrous claim. Because there's a lot of stuff out there to make us cautious and afraid: all the shootings by random gunmen at schools and even in churches; rising unemployment rates; the rise of identity theft; and 9/11 always in the back of our national imagination. I read recently that doctors are ordering more expensive medical tests than ever before because patients are demanding them, sometimes without any obvious symptom to warrant the test. Many things make us wary and cautious, fretful and afraid. We tend to really trust only a handful of people. And sometimes we wonder about them.

Jesus could tinker around with his life, live sacrificially for others, and stand up to darkness and principalities—how exactly? Because he was blessed with supernatural powers to zap the bad guys, right? No. His *identity* was absolutely clear. "He had come from God, and was going to God."

When we truly understand that this is also our gift—that nothing can get us, nothing can ultimately harm us because God has claimed us—then we too are freed and empowered to love as Jesus loved. If we too are born of God, then the love we give away will always be replenished by a God to whom we are returning. If our identity is intact, if we are indeed returning to God, then absolutely nothing can interrupt this destiny. Nothing at all can ultimately "get" you, because (hear this again) God's already got you. Jesus knew these very basic facts throughout his ministry, as he radically loved others and as he faced the events of Holy Week.

Second, it strikes me in this old story that washing feet (radical love, in other words) and eating supper are two intimately related events. Jesus rises from the table, pours water into a basin, and washes feet. Supper and service go hand in hand. Foot washing was the absolute height of grunt work in Jesus's day—sort of like scrubbing a toilet or scooping up dog droppings from your backyard. Nobody volunteered for these things.

There is no formal institution of the Eucharist in the Gospel of John. But John wants us to clearly see the connection between eating and serving. In the fourth century, Saint Augustine preached a powerful sermon about the Eucharist. As people stretched out their hands for the sacrament, he said, "Become what you receive." We receive the body of Christ and become the body of Christ in the same action. Jesus was aware of the profound connection between eating and serving. As we receive the mystery of his body and blood, his love powerfully courses through the church's veins, spilling through our lives to others. We are able to love as Jesus loved only because he sustains us with heavenly food. Try serving in Christ's name (as he loved) without this food. I'm fairly sure you will not be at it for very long.

Third, it is absolutely remarkable to me that Jesus knew of Judas's intentions that night, but he still ate with the traitorous guy anyway. And he still tenderly washed the man's feet. Verse 11: "Jesus knew who was to betray him." I have always felt that Judas has unfairly played the role of church whipping boy down through the centuries. The truth is that I am Judas; you are Judas. I betray Jesus all the time. The remarkable thing here is that Jesus makes no attempt whatsoever to drive out evil, misguided people from his midst. Instead, he dines with them and even washes their feet. When Jesus says, "Love one another, as I have loved you," it's vitally important to remember that this love is not just for the deserving and upstanding. We can only love this radically merciful way as we recall Jesus's forgiveness of our own Judas-like behavior.

"Love one another," he says. How? You know. It's that devastating little word: *as* I have loved you. As I say, I really wouldn't blame anyone for running out the church door at the hearing of these words. But if you choose to stay and live out the implications of this little adverb, here's how. Identity. Meal. Mercy.

"Love one another," he says, "*just as I have loved you.*" It sounds impossible, but if we watch Jesus (the master teacher) closely, he shows us exactly how.

● ● ●

More than at any other time of my quarter-century-spanning ministry, I feel that Satan is real. The Father of Lies lives in ways that are not easily discernible. It's almost laughable that one of the names for this evil entity is Lucifer—literally, "bearer of light." It's sometimes very difficult to discern light from darkness. A protracted process of adult conversion must be in place in congregational life to shape new ministry leaders who are dealing with very old temptations that can only be overcome with equally old stories of courage, truth, and good news.

In the chapters that follow, I will describe how easy it is to lie and tell half-truths in pastoral ministry. The loving truth of Christ is of vital importance in the normal rounds of weekly pastoral leadership and ministry as we encounter the reality of a compelling false voice that entices clergy to entertain the possibility of shortcuts and deceit. Thank goodness that we are not sent out alone. One is praying for pastors like me even now: "Righteous Father, the world does not know you, but I know you; and these know that you have sent me. I made your name known to them, and I will make it known, so that the love with which you have loved me may be in them, and I in them" (John 17:25–26).

PART 2

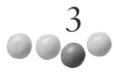

3

Honesty in Preaching

The Pulpit as Witness Stand

The preacher preaches out of love for her people, and what she preaches is the love of God. There is no better way to love a congregation than to preach truth to them, and central to that truth is the love of God in Jesus Christ. It is not easy love or cheap love, but it is the love that shaped creation, fashioned the people Israel, was incarnate in the man Jesus, continues to sustain the church, and drives history towards its consummation.[1]

David Bartlett

We have this hope, a sure and steadfast anchor of the soul, a hope that enters the inner shrine behind the curtain, where Jesus, a forerunner on our behalf, has entered.

Hebrews 6:19–20

I liked Pastor's sermon because he is not kidding about what he is trying to say to us all.[2]

nine-year-old worshiper in Kentucky

The first part of this book examined life in the local parish and our common encounter with three biblical realities: Satan (the Father of Lies); Jesus's radical invitation to baptismal renunciation of the devil; and our Lord's call to live a holy and lifelong truth (conversion). The next five chapters will look at several pastoral roles—preaching, pastoral counseling, teaching, funerals, and church council leadership—within the context of the beloved community (church) and through the lens of clergy truth telling. As in part 1, I'll speak specifically through my own ongoing conversion to Christ as a pastor called by God to this odd vocation. Keep in mind that any lens on this side of the grave is cloudy and stained with sin. "For now we see in a mirror, dimly"[3] (1 Cor. 13:12). As these chapters unfold, pastors (myself in particular) should recall wisdom from the book of Hebrews: "Every high priest chosen from among mortals is put in charge of things pertaining to God on their behalf, to offer gifts and sacrifices for sins. He is able to deal gently with the ignorant and wayward, since he himself is subject to weakness" (5:1–2). I'm no high priest, but I've got the "subject to weakness" part down pat.

Preaching and Plagiarism

Tom Long, professor of preaching at Candler School of Theology in Atlanta, was in town a couple of Novembers ago for a speaking engagement at Ebenezer Church. The pastoral staff treated Tom to dinner that Thursday evening at the Blue Marlin on Lincoln Street. The street, named for good old "Honest Abe," turned out to be a poignant venue for sharing truth. As the salads arrived, I recalled a 2007 article about preaching and plagiarism that Tom had written for the *Christian Century*. There he had named a problem plaguing the church in a new way since the advent of the internet: pirating some or even all of someone else's sermon and allowing the material to pose as one's own writing and original thought. Preachers of my own acquaintance have been caught delivering sermons swiped word for word from cyberspace. Tom had written persuasively:

> Perhaps as much or more than any other form of communication, preaching depends upon a cord of trust binding together the speaker and the listener, the preacher and the hearer. A good sermon consists not primarily in flawless logic, soaring poetry or airtight arguments, but in passionately held truth proclaimed with conviction. To compromise the truth in ways that hearers would consider deceptive makes them reluctant to extend this necessary trust and damages the witness.[4]

Tom shared that evening over dinner another conversation he'd had with a pastor who reacted to his article in a negative way: "What's the big deal, Dr. Long? We're getting the message of the gospel out, aren't we?" Tom's response: "The big deal? Well, in short, you're lying while your congregation thinks you're telling the truth."

This conversation was rather fresh for me, as I'd recently been disappointed by a certain publisher[5] who had swiped my own series of sermons, transmitting them electronically, without payment (breaking a contract) or specific permission. The owner of the company consistently refused to answer my emails when questioned. How have we come to this? A friend of Long comments on the insatiable hunger among desperate preachers searching for last-minute inspiration: "The Internet is like having a drug dealer on every corner."[6]

> Only preachers who deliver their own sermons stand with one foot in the life of the people and one foot in the biblical text. No Internet preacher stands in this same place. No borrowed sermon, however fine, can answer the question that cries out from every congregation, "Is there a word today, a word for us,

from the Lord?" This is not the same as saying that sermons must be fully original. All preachers borrow from others, and should. There is a difference between being a debtor and a thief. All preachers stand on the shoulders of biblical scholars, theologians and faithful witnesses from across the generations. We do not owe our congregations an original essay; we owe them a fresh act of interpretation.[7]

Preachers, of course, are as prone as parishioners to fall headlong into the surrounding culture—formed by television, web immersion, and myriad shortcuts—instead of the living Word. It's easy to graduate from seminary and get tugged each week hither and yon by competing needs and concerns that have little to do with our primary calling. Suddenly it's Saturday night and we have nothing to say. If pastors are honest about how we spend our time, this loss for words should not surprise us.

After acknowledging our common tendency to become "dull in understanding" (Heb. 5:11) and needing "milk, not solid food" (5:12), the author of Hebrews challenges the church to leave behind "the basic teaching about Christ" (6:1) and move on to more mature and advanced theological subjects. I suspect most preachers who rely on internet sermons and other deceptive shortcuts have stopped their quest for wisdom in Christ. Often the issue is not so much that we're harried and out of time. It's a matter of priorities and letting others set an agenda for us. Again, please be clear: the devil can use these excuses to stunt effective proclamation of the gospel and the growth of the Holy Spirit (conversion) within individual pastors.

Truth in the Midst of Suffering

Perhaps you'll find a couple hours sometime soon to see what I think is one of the most overlooked movies of 2008—*Defi-*

ance starring Daniel Craig. The story (based on actual events) is set largely in a forest in Poland, as fearful Jews flee the Nazis and try to forge a makeshift community deep in the woods. The group is constantly moving just like their biblical forebears. They deal with lack of food, horrible weather, and illness as they relocate and rebuild again and again in an effort to find a safe place to live. They struggle with issues of leadership, whether or not to use violence, and internal spats. They wonder if God has abandoned them.

There is a character in the movie, Shamon Haretz, a university professor, who serves as the community rabbi. He presides at a wedding in the forest and, of course, over funerals. Over a grave, he prays, "Merciful God, we commit our friends to you. We have no more prayers, no more tears; we have run out of blood. Choose another people. We have paid for each of our commandments; we have covered every stone and field with ashes. Sanctify another land. Choose another people. Teach them the deeds and the prophecies. Grant us but one more gift: take away our holiness. Amen." It's an honest prayer. Holiness, of course, gets in the way of a lot of possible options, right?

As the story unfolded, I couldn't help but think what I would do as a leader in similar circumstances. What would any pastor do if our lovely buildings burned down and we were threatened and forced to move quickly? What would hold a congregation together? But at movie's end I mostly pondered how very insulated I am from the world's suffering. What really captivates my attention most days? I left the theater with an odd mixture of embarrassment and thanksgiving.

Listening to Jesus

Mark's version of the transfiguration of Jesus (Mark 9:2–8) begins with an odd reference to time: "Six days later, Jesus

59

took with him Peter and James and John, and led them up a high mountain apart, by themselves" (9:2). I guess they concluded that whatever Jesus was talking about six days ago was blessedly behind them now. Maybe the Lord was sort of addled when he told the disciples—just a handful of verses before this mountain junket—that very soon he would suffer, be rejected by the elders, and be killed (8:31). There was an ugly little spat between Peter and Jesus (8:32–33) about that sacrificial prediction and the direction the community should now take. A good bit of tension swirled through the air as that scene concluded.

But six days pass and all that now seems to be behind them. Jesus leads three of his pals (all fishermen, please recall) up a high mountain. And if this is Mount Hermon, as most scholars think, then it took awhile to ascend 9,230 feet to the mountain's peak. And the fishermen, used to the air and terrain of sea level, are probably winded and sprawling in an open meadow with peanuts, raisins, and a water bottle—close to two miles higher than the nets they left back on the beach.

So they really aren't looking at Jesus at first, are they? They're sucking air and rather giddy to have made it, sort of relieved that Jesus seems to have calmed down from his nutty speech six days before and all that stuff about sacrifice. And when the displaced fishermen do look up through the mist, they see a dazzling Jesus talking with two Old Testament heroes. Peter, true to vocation, tries to net them, so to speak.

In Mark's version, the story never says exactly what these giants of the faith are talking about—broadly about his departure (*exodus* in the Greek) in Luke 9:31—but I like to think that maybe Jesus was seeking advice from Moses about how in the dickens he managed to lead six hundred thousand

Israelites[8] through the desert for forty years, when Jesus was having so much difficulty leading just the twelve.

Nor are we informed about the conversation with Elijah, but isn't it rather neat that after God swings low with the chariot to nab Elijah (2 Kings 2:9–12) so many years prior, we don't hear from the slippery little prophet again in the Bible—until now. The chariot presumably bounces around the heavens for several centuries before finally landing on this very mountain and depositing Elijah into the conversation. After his journey, the prophet could have written the consummate *Hitchhiker's Guide to the Galaxy.*

Bible stories like these cause my friends outside the church to say things like, "Well, I see they tried to nab Michael Phelps for smoking a certain substance in your town. But I have to ask you, Frank, if there wasn't also something growing on top of Mount Hermon that affected the content of the story you're asking me to swallow here. Please, what are you doing with your life?"

Let's just say, in reply, that people who take God seriously will indeed hitchhike back and forth between centuries; *then* shaping now, and *now* never forgetting then—our very lives imprinted by these stories so powerfully that we too are caught up in the whirlwind of biblical promise. We learn from the stories how to build community in the forest, desert, or wherever we happen to wander.

If Jesus could produce bread for five thousand (and then four thousand more) in the days just before this hike, then I suppose it was not beyond the realm of Peter's imagination to think his Lord could suddenly produce a hammer and nails at ninety-two-hundred feet above sea level. "He did not know *what* to say," the story says of Peter (Mark 9:6). This erstwhile fisherman, far from his nets, probably speaks for us all. Faced with mystery and awe, he wants to build something. (Maybe that's why many pastors are more interested in building programs than the tough weekly work of exegesis.) I think it's very interesting that God puts the kibosh on the first church building program until the disciples get straight the mission of Jesus. We sometimes reverse that order.

The voice is quite clear on this: "This is my Son, the Beloved; listen to him" (Mark 9:7). *Listen to him.* It's our first and primary task as the church. Listen to Jesus—first, always first. That's a tough teaching. For Americans like me, putting Jesus first is difficult. We are people with omnivorous desire. Even though we may be cutting back in these "tough economic times," I wonder how the recession will really change most of us. As a character in one of Flannery O'Connor's novels puts it, "Nobody with a good car needs to be justified."[9] It's tempting to seek "justification" in a hundred places other than Jesus.

Those on the mountain that day are "overshadowed" (Mark 9:7) by God. Lord help us, but that's exactly what we preachers need—to be overshadowed. Gaining elevation, these first preachers probably figured that what Jesus was talking about six days ago was all behind them now. Time for a nice little shortcut to the truth and the reward of the gospel. But in reality, sacrifice was ahead of them; it would become their way of life—the way of the cross. To find our lives, we lose them in the way of Jesus (Mark 8:35).

Being Overshadowed by the Spirit

I'm intrigued by the use of the word *overshadowed* in the transfiguration story and wonder if you also recall another instance of this word in the call of a certain virgin who willingly risked reputation to carry the infant Jesus. "The Holy Spirit will come upon you, and the power of the Most High will overshadow you; therefore the child to be born will be holy; he will be called Son of God" (Luke 1:35). Phillips Brooks in his 1877 Yale lectures coined the phrase "Preaching is truth through personality."[10] Here in the early twenty-first century, however, we are awash in television preaching personalities and need more truth that overshadows homiletic reputation and popularity. Perhaps the real place for truthful preaching is always between Mary's gestational humility and Peter's wilderness fear on the mountain. Both personalities were overshadowed by the Holy Spirit, who brought a message that gave birth to courage and discipleship. Mary, if you think about it, was Jesus's first disciple. Peter was perhaps his boldest. Both personalities were demoted, then molded and shaped by surprising and unexpected revelation.

Maybe preachers take homiletical shortcuts via the internet because we suspect the Holy Spirit no longer speaks in this wild and overshadowing way. Or we may be afraid that if we are open to God, the Spirit might grab us and take us somewhere against our will. There's a lot at stake in faithful preaching.

I've been thinking about a recent email from my friend Ron Luckey, a Lutheran campus minister during my student days at Clemson. Luckey writes, "Most pastors and laity understand pastoral relationships as personal. Therefore, when the pastor speaks truth folks 'take it personally' and often head for the door. I was not taught in seminary that, 'in truth,' pastoral relationships with parishioners are public relationships based on accomplishing together a mission even when that mission is personally offensive and potentially abrasive relationally."[11] Avoiding the hurt Ron describes here may not be entirely possible. But there might be a better outcome for all concerned if pastors like me would regularly ponder the nature of the Spirit that "overshadows" personality without quite swallowing it. What would happen if pastors truly believed the basic and biblical truth that "God is first in the pulpit and I am not"? I am blessedly (and fearfully) overshadowed by that confession.

Five Components of Truthful Preaching

Once properly overshadowed by the Spirit and bathed in holy prayer, the pastor can face expectantly the weekly preaching task with fresh eyes, ears, and heart. What might a truthful homiletic look like? I offer five suggestions for this important and vital pastoral role of preaching God's truth in love. Please remember: it is a profoundly difficult challenge to preach overshadowed. To incorporate the humility of Mary and the fear of Peter into the way you live the Word is no small task. Please don't assume I'm anywhere near pulling it off on a regular basis. Like old Zechariah, I'm regularly rendered mute while tending the holy of holies (Luke 1:19–20). I tiptoe only so far into the text, assuming easy inspiration will arrive by week's end. Faithful exegesis is always hard work. There have also been Sundays when I've wanted to vomit before and after the delivery of the sermon. Faithful exegesis can get you killed (see Luke 4:29–30). Honest preaching (as David Bartlett suggests in the quotation opening this chapter) is ultimately offered out of love born in our common baptism, a love that is never easy or cheap. This truthful love can create a new world.

Imagine yourself preparing to preach as we ponder together the nature of truthful proclamation. Better yet, imagine yourself in your very place of preaching with Pastor John Ames, the likeable minister in Marilynne Robinson's novel *Gilead*:

> Then, if I woke up still in my armchair, and if the clock said four or five, I'd think how pleasant it was to walk through the streets in the dark and let myself into the church and watch

dawn come in the sanctuary. I loved the sound of the latch lifting. The building has settled into itself so that when you walk down the aisle, you can hear it yielding to the burden of your weight. It's a pleasanter sound than an echo would be, an obliging, accommodating sound. You have to be there alone to hear it. . . . After a while I did begin to wonder if I liked the church better with no people in it.[12]

Also, try to think of specific faces slowly filling that quiet space. Recall the encouragement of Ezekiel: "And you, O mortal, do not be afraid of them, and do not be afraid of their words, though briers and thorns surround you and you live among scorpions; do not be afraid of their words, and do not be dismayed at their looks, for they are a rebellious house" (Ezek. 2:6). I suspect there is a direct relationship between our fear of conflict and the tendency to preach half-truths and take homiletical shortcuts.

Proclamation from the Grave

For many months now I've been intrigued by a strange passage from early Exodus that will never make it into the Sunday lectionary. To recap: God hounds Moses, in spite of the would-be prophet's myriad excuses and liabilities, until Moses says, "Okay, but I really don't want to go. Can't you find somebody else?" Moses and his family set out for Egypt, but "on the way, at a place where they spent the night, the Lord met [Moses] and tried to kill him" (Exod. 4:24). Luckily, the fast-thinking Zipporah cuts off their son's foreskin, wipes the bloody mess on her husband's feet, and this seems to change God's mind about the planned murder (4:25–26). Have you ever noticed this strange passage? Please help me out here: what does it mean?

I've asked biblical scholars (and many pastors) this question, and all are tongue-tied. I've finally concluded that any-

65

one who speaks for God must be not only overshadowed but actually "killed" before presuming to speak truth to power. In gospel terms, all truthful preaching must be inherently baptismal, reflecting honestly about the nature of the preacher's drowning, death, and resurrection in the graceful waters (Rom. 6:1–14).[13] So yes, think overshadowing here in Exodus, but also think foreshadowing of our baptismal dying and rising. All honest preaching is ultimately not the idea of the preacher but rather God's nutty agenda. I would not sign up voluntarily for a job that would stick my neck on the line before Pharaoh, so God's going to have to kill and raise me first.

Pastors escape in many ways. We exercise shoddy exegesis under the guise of busyness and church business. We tell nice little cut-and-paste stories about World War II or "little Timmy the handicapped boy," throwing the congregation a bone of innocuous sweetness and light. "Because pulpit storytelling is a dress rehearsal for the living of the Christian life," writes Tom Long, "this means that it is ethically irresponsible to tell the canned and simplistic preacher stories that drain away the moral and theological ambiguities inherent in real life. Preacher stories that always yield the right moral lesson or end up in triumph without struggle are a damned lie about human life and Christian faith."[14] David Bartlett lampoons the famous train story in which a father pulls a "bloody switch" to sacrifice his little son so that those on the train might live. "Even if this actually happened," writes Bartlett, "it does not illumine the way real lives need to respond to the real God, and thus it is not gospel. It is *Guideposts* on a bad day."[15]

I read somewhere that early Christians would often share the Eucharist over the grave of a beloved saint who had just died, often passing the elements back and forth over the open resting place of the dearly departed. Perhaps preaching should also retain a similar image—the congregation buried in baptism; the preacher standing at the entrance to the open tomb; the Holy Spirit providing the words to take a few feeble steps into the unknown land of promise. Jesus speaks not only to Lazarus but to the collective bound community: "Unbind [them], let [them] go" (John 11:44).

The Importance of Entry Points

Pastors have the attention of the congregation as the sermon opens, and it's very easy to lose that attention in the first thirty seconds. Entry points are vital in the success of any sermon. Our attention to them should not so much strive for cuteness but rather set the tone that something of great importance will be considered in the next fifteen minutes. A revealing task for pastors might be to critically examine the last ten introductions we've penned for Sunday sermons. Can the conclusion and content of a sermon clearly refer back to the introduction? Is the text of the day emerging clearly or at least through allusion? Is the introduction interesting, timely, and not fluffy or canned? Here are several introductions from my own sermons. Try to match the introduction with the scriptural passages that follow.

A. One can look at this little skirmish between prophets this morning and think, "My gosh, these people were nuts." One man of God verbally attacks another. One man of prayer goes after another with all the ferocity of a Jerry Springer episode. Wooden yokes are smashed to smithereens. Pushing, shoving, death threats ensue. The situation would be like me getting into an argument, a shoving match, right here in the chancel with Pastor Paul, throwing a chalice of wine in his face, wrestling him to the floor, and ripping off his robe, shouting, "Impostor! Impostor pastor!"

B. I have a good friend who once told me, "You Christians always want to talk about sin. 'Jesus died to forgive our sins.' Sin, sin, sin. Come on, get over it. What does it really matter that a man supposedly died for my sins? That was such a long time ago and this is now. Did that make God happy or something? That his Son died on a cross for what I and countless others did and would do? Did that appease the Big Guy—somebody taking the rap for the world's screwups? I just don't understand Christians. Why is the whole notion of sin so important to you, Frank? Especially if God goes ahead and forgives everything anyway?"

C. In May of 1981, a young couple was shot and murdered in a shelter in southwest Virginia on the Appalachian Trail moments after they fed a stranger a meal. Their bodies were buried in the woods. I remember this incident because I was hiking that whole year and actually spent the night in that same shelter only weeks before the crime occurred. When I heard the news, it spooked me—not only because I'd left a logbook (no doubt confiscated by the state police) in that very shelter but also because the crime shook the normally peaceful hiking community all the way from Maine to Georgia. Crime is very rare on the Appalachian Trail. You're much more likely to encounter crime in your own neighborhood here in Columbia. They caught the murderer in Myrtle Beach a few weeks later. Randall Lee Smith, an emotionally troubled man who'd been abused as a child, was sentenced to a very long jail term through a plea bargain arranged with the families of the victims. I haven't thought about this a whole lot in the twenty-seven years that have passed since that crime. But last week a friend pointed me to a series of articles in the *Washington Post*. An attempted murder, a shooting, occurred this past May (two months ago) in that same mountainous area very close to that same shelter. This time, thankfully, the victims lived. Unbelievably, the assailant was the same Randall Lee Smith. A model prisoner, he'd been released from prison and paroled several years before.

D. There was a knock, I'll grant that. But a half hour before the knock there was a man slipping into the shadows, nervously ducking into back alleys, pulling up a hood to cover his head. He is nervous, this man, furtively tossing a glance over a shoulder, doubly careful to make sure no one is following. He watches the candles go out one by one in his neighborhood, waiting as people turn in for the night. And for a second, finally arriving at his destination, he can't quite tell if anyone is still up. But yes, there in the back of the house—clear, unmistakable light.

E. I no longer ask a certain question to young couples who come to me for pre-wedding counseling sessions. I no longer ask them *why* they want to get married. I used to ask that question, and couples would invariably look at me as if I was some sort of certified dolt, ready for institutional life. "Why, we're in love, pastor," they'd say. But that favorite four-letter word always came out as if poured from a bottle of maple syrup, in slow motion. Our notions of love have been shaped largely by Hallmark and Cupid—we confuse love with whatever makes the heart go pitter-patter.

Can you match the introduction with its Scripture passage?

_____ "For in gathering the weeds, you would uproot the wheat along with them" (Matt. 13:29).

_____ "For I do not do what I want, but I do the very thing I hate" (Rom. 7:15).

_____ "Listen, Hananiah, the Lord has not sent you, and you made this people trust in a lie" (Jer. 28:15).

_____ "Now there was a Pharisee named Nicodemus, a leader of the Jews. He came to Jesus by night" (John 3:1–2).

_____ "Love is not envious or boastful or arrogant or rude. It does not insist on its own way" (1 Cor. 13:4–5).

The introductions I've shared here are not cited as stunning examples of the art of preaching. But an effective introduction should keep the congregation's attention, connect clearly to the preached text, and telegraph that we'll all be dealing with truth—and perhaps unveiling a common lie or two along the way—in the moments to come.[16]

Learning from Poetry

My friend Ron Rash, a South Carolina poet and fiction writer, has a poem titled "Under Jocassee."[17] An abiding theme in all of Ron's fiction and poetry is the recovery of hidden cultures and their important intersection with a modern world that often speeds past lost wisdom without a second thought. The grandson of descendants who settled in Watauga and Buncombe Counties of North Carolina, Ron consistently plumbs the depth, beauty, and challenges of forgotten mountain communities now known largely for tourism. Craig Barnes, in his wonderful book, *The Pastor as Minor Poet*, writes:

> The purpose of poetry is to reveal the mystery and the miracle that lie beneath the ordinary. It doesn't argue, buttress against

doubt, or defend. It explores. Then it unveils what it finds in voices such as awe, wonder, irony, or even anger and lament rather than instruction or debate. Poets are seldom accused of being convincing, but the best ones can transform the way we see life. . . . Poets never use illustrations, but they often invoke powerful images. The difference between them is that an illustration is typically an ornament that hangs on the sermon, while an image is always a compelling picture that invites the beholder to look through it into the greater mystery.[18]

In the Rash poem cited above, the reader boards a small boat on a beautiful, cloudless day, paddles along the shoreline of Lake Jocassee in upstate South Carolina, and peers down into the water toward a road (now submerged) that once connected residents to other remote mountain communities. The poem then recedes in time and imagination to a past decade before the flooding of the valley created the lake. A woman walks from her barn near the road and "suddenly shivers" from a shadowy darkness mistaken for a cloud blocking the sun. By the conclusion of the poem, one realizes the shadow is actually cast by the boat on the surface of the water; time is bridged between the woman's dark premonition and the deep gaze of the reader.

When our three children were young, they used to love Michael Ende's book *The Never-Ending Story*. Later made into an American movie, *The Never-Ending Story* tells of the adventures of little Bastian, a boy alienated from his own world at school. Bastian finds himself somehow actually transported from his school world into the world of the book he is reading. The events of the book seem to be calling out to him for action. When he pulls back, Bastian discovers the plot of the story turns in on itself and cannot proceed any further. Only when Bastian makes a decision to become part of the book's story does his real world at school begin to make any sense at all.

Poets and fiction writers have much to teach preachers in terms of timing, imagery, narrative, and colorful language. The best novelists and poets are doing what the best sermons are attempting to do: helping the listeners see their lives in the story. Unedited truth can often crush a person under its weight. Poets guide the reader into the arena of truth without overly explaining the point. A good sermon ideally works this same way. The danger, of course, is that the listener never makes the connective leap from image to truth. Or that the connective leap made by the listener may be so far from what the preacher intended as to leave a pastor scratching her head. But the risk is worth it. Poets are tapping into the way Jesus shared truth with his listeners—elliptically. Poetic truth telling allows God's truth to surprise and stick with listeners in a world in which we're used to hearing (and telling) so many lies and half-truths.

Truth and Theodicy

Roger Rosenblatt, master of the short essay and longtime contributor to *Time* magazine, writes powerfully about the death of his daughter:

> Road rage was a danger those first weeks. I picked fights with store clerks for no reason. I lost my temper with a student who phoned me too frequently about her work. I seethed at those who spoke of Amy's death in the clichés of modern usage, such as "passing" and "closure." I cursed God. In a way, believing in God made Amy's death more, not less, comprehensible, since the God I believe in is not beneficent. He doesn't care. A friend was visiting Jerusalem when he got the news about Amy. He kicked the Wailing Wall, and said, "F--- you, God!" My sentiments exactly.[19]

Since pastors so often walk in and out of tragedy and human suffering, I've often wondered why more don't lose their faith and just chuck church altogether. And for those who cannot help but remain, I'm curious why they don't give voice to the doubts and struggles concerning God and suffering that are surely rampant in the pews each Sunday.

My son, Lukas, was recently involved in a very serious auto accident in which he could easily have died. He fell asleep and hit a brick wall at 5:00 a.m., moments after dropping off his spring prom date at her house. If you want to discover what someone truly believes about God, hop into the backseat of their car as they speed toward the site of an accident, not knowing whether their son is dead or alive.

The 911 dispatcher had said, "Your son is injured. An ambulance is on its way." "He's hurt? How bad?" I ask in a sleepy stupor. "Yes, he's hurt. I don't know the extent of the injury." "Is anyone with him?" "No," she said. "He called us on his cell phone. An ambulance is en route." I suspect most people in a similar circumstance would offer a few prayers like mine in the car on the way: *Please, God! I'll do better— better dad, better husband, better friend, better pastor. Just please. I'll do anything!* When we arrived at the scene of the accident, we couldn't see Lukas, only the mangled automobile, some flashing lights, and an ambulance. And then a policeman, running—running toward us with the best news we could ever hear. "He's gonna be okay. He'll be all right. He's gonna live."

Bill Maher, in his wickedly satirical movie, *Religulous*, converses with a true believer about prayer. Maher sarcastically wonders why we've given up a jolly man who delivers presents to so many each December and not another who somehow hears all our intercessions: "Of course, Santa Claus is ridiculous. One man hearing every murmur at the same time? That, I get." Annie Dillard seriously poses a similar concern in her beguiling book, *For the Time Being*: "Now the notion of God the Semipotent has trickled down to the theologian in the street. . . . God is no more blinding people with glaucoma, or testing them with diabetes, or purifying them with spinal pain, or choreographing the seeding of tumor cells through lymph, or fiddling with chromosomes, than he is jimmying floodwaters or pitching tornadoes at towns. . . . Then what, if anything, does he do? If God does not cause everything that happens, does God cause anything that happens? Is God completely out of the loop?"[20]

I'm afraid many of our church members are, at best, semi-literate. I've often been dismayed that even church leaders in the Lutheran tradition have difficulty describing the difference between the book of Numbers and the book of Galatians. But this is not to say that those who show up Sunday after Sunday are disinterested when it comes to struggling with important and befuddling theological issues like the presence or absence of God in the midst of tragedy. Giving voice to such theological confusion is a very faithful (and biblical) way to encounter many lectionary texts.

God's representatives in popular television outlets regularly say strange things about God. I came across an essay not long ago written by the popular preacher John Piper. Pastor Piper is trying to make sense of the famous plane crash in the Hudson River in January of 2009 in which Captain Sullenberger saved the day and landed the plane safely:

> Have you considered how unlikely was the crash of USAir flight 1549 in the Hudson River on January 15—not just the rescue but the crash itself? Picture this: The Airbus A320 is taking off at an angle—maybe 30 degrees. It's not flying horizontal with the earth. Not only that, it is flying fast—not full speed yet, but perhaps four times as fast as your car would go at top highway speeds. The geese are flying horizontally with the ground, more or less. They are not flying in a cloud like a swarm of bees. They fly level with the ground, often shaped

like a V. In view of all that, what are the odds that, traveling at this speed and at this angle, this airplane would intersect with the flight of those geese at that very millisecond which would put a bird not just in one of those engines, but both of them? Two laser-guided missiles would not have been as amazingly effective as were those geese. It is incredible, statistically speaking. If God governs nature down to the fall (and the flight) of every bird, as Jesus says (Matt. 10:29), then the crash of flight 1549 was designed by God. . . . If God guides geese so precisely, he also guides the captain's hands. God knew that when he took the plane down, he would also give a spectacular deliverance. So why would he do that? If he means for all to live, why not just skip the crash? Because he meant to give our nation a parable of his power and mercy the week before a new President takes office.[21]

Wow. And I cannot imagine, using this logic, what God meant to demonstrate later that same month when a flight in Buffalo crashed and killed everyone on board.

I do not pretend to know the answers to faith-shaking questions posed at the time of tragedy and suffering. I can only imagine what my faith response might have been if my son, Lukas, had been killed in his post-prom crash. But I do know that preachers in their sermons need to be careful not to pretend to know the will of God in all befuddling incidents. My first reaction upon reading Piper's essay was to wish he had kept his thoughts to himself.

But what do we say? How can sermons honestly tell the truth about agonizing incidents that seem to have no point?

Weeks before my son's accident, but only a couple after Obama's inauguration and Piper's essay, I ran across a short story by one of my favorite writers, Ron Hansen.[22] The story oddly also centers upon a plane crash, birds, and the death of a young mother who apparently did not have someone as skillful as Captain Chesley B. Sullenberger in the cockpit with her in the flight lessons that went terribly awry. Most of the story captures the reaction of the children, twelve-year-old Aidan and fifteen-year-old Lucy, who mourn the death of their mom.

> Aidan once wandered into the bedroom he still thought of as his mother's though only his father slept there now. Nothing had changed since September. His mother's clothing still hung in the closet—a faint hint of her sweat in her gardening shirt, a faint trace of Chanel in a cocktail dress. And hair was still in her hairbrush; her creams, conditioners, and cleansing lotions were like a cityscape on the mirrored counter in the master bathroom.[23]

Aidan's grief for his mom leads him to the door of Father Jim Schwartz, the assistant pastor in their congregation.

> "She was really nice," Aidan said. "She never did anything wrong."
> Sins of his own started vagrantly populating his thoughts.
> "And you're wondering why she died?"
> "Sort of."
> The priest's right elbow was on the arm of the chair and his right cheek was against his knuckles, as in a book-jacket photograph illustrating wise consideration. "The psalmists asked it long ago," he said. "Why do the evil prosper? Why do the innocent suffer? Why, when a loved one is dying, doesn't God intercede? Those are philosophical questions and they fall under a category called 'theodicy.'"
> "I'm just twelve," Aidan said.[24]

The awkward conversation between adult and child continues. Aidan admits that the priest has helped. "I guess just talking. . . . Hearing about other people." Time passes in the story, and Aidan's father visits his son's classroom to talk about his job as an accountant. A sparrow flies through an open window. Children and teacher swat at the bird and

try to shoo the frightened sparrow out. Finally, Aidan's dad
suggests that the class quietly leave the room and maybe the
bird will calm down and find its own way. The story ends on
a haunting and beautiful note:

> The sparrow calmed and cruised the four corners of the
> classroom until it felt the chill from the foot-high opening
> in an upper window and with a sudden swerve was flying
> into the immensity of outdoors. . . . Aidan filed back inside
> with the others. His father never mentioned it, and Aidan
> didn't tell Lucy because he wanted it for himself: that feeling
> of friendship with the silence he had been hearing but had
> not understood.[25]

Although I much prefer Hansen's short story to Piper's anx-
ious effort to make sense of every tragic detail, there still remains *some truth* for the preacher to proclaim using words, for
"we proclaim Christ crucified, a stumbling block to Jews and
foolishness to Gentiles, but to those who are the called, both
Jews and Greeks, Christ the power of God and the wisdom
of God" (1 Cor. 1:23–24). Preachers dare to enter the silence
with fear and trepidation, not to explain the unexplainable
but to proclaim a Christ who hangs alongside us in our own
crucifying moments. We need to be careful not to say too much
here, but we also need to be careful not to say too little.

Part of my own silence in the face of suffering is related
to something more than simply not wanting to be thrown
together with pastors like John Piper (though I'm sure the
man has many good things to say beyond his comments on
the goose crash over the Hudson). My silence about suffering
is also related to the fact that I'm relatively insulated from
it, even though I wade into suffering more than most North
Americans. Paul Farmer, a doctor who has devoted his life
to providing medical care for the poor in Haiti and other
impoverished countries, has much to say to people like me:

The fact that any sort of religious faith was disdained at Harvard and so important to the poor—not just in Haiti but elsewhere, too—made me even more convinced that faith must be something good. . . . I know it sounds shallow, the opiate thing, needing to believe, palliating pain, but it didn't feel shallow. It was more profound than other sentiments I'd known, and I was taken with the idea that in an ostensibly godless world that worshiped money and power or, more seductively, a sense of personal efficacy and advancement, like at Duke and Harvard, there was still a place to look for God, and that was in the suffering of the poor. You want to talk crucifixion? I'll show you crucifixion, you bastards.[26]

I may never go to Haiti, and the people with whom I "proclaim Christ crucified" may not suffer as dreadfully as many others, but as a preacher I can use narrative as "a means for remembering the lost and silenced," as Tom Long puts it, "to keep alive in the church's memory the stories of those whose lives are not remembered and celebrated and truthfully narrated elsewhere in our culture."[27] To "believe in the communion of saints" is to acknowledge a large canon of stories that the preacher can access without having lived them. "If one member suffers, all suffer together with it; if one member is honored, all rejoice together with it" (1 Cor. 12:26).

The Wideness of God's Mercy

When I was in the third grade, a young friend introduced me to the concept of hell. Somehow I'd been shielded from all talk about the locus of everlasting torment. Perhaps my Lutheran parents were staunch in their sharing of doctrine that focused primarily on a God of grace and love. I don't know. Anyway, hell had somehow escaped my eight-year-old attention.

My friend took care of that. In vivid detail he laid out the hazards of living a less-than-upright life. God, I was informed, could do more than love you. He could also "get" you and send you to a place too uncomfortable to bear. Hell was for bad people, he would say, so I didn't have to worry.

I did worry, though—and deeply. Especially after we had an argument one afternoon and he told me to go there, which *did* tarnish his credentials as an authority on hell just a bit because he'd just told me that only God made such decisions.

Jesus describes a separation, a judgment, a final reckoning in the New Testament. In the parable of the ten bridesmaids (Matt. 25:1–13), five run out of oil. They knock and knock on the door and ask to enter the banquet hall. Request denied. In the parable of the sheep and the goats, we read, "Whenever you refused to help one of these little ones," says the King, "you refused to help me" (Matt. 25:31–46). Some are sent away to eternal punishment, others to eternal life.

But then there are other words from Jesus that suggest his saving cross will be universal: "And I," says Jesus, "when I am lifted up from the earth, will draw *all people* to myself" (John 12:32). He doesn't say he'll draw just his kind of people, or just those who've been good girls and boys, or only those who've never been caught at anything. The word is *all*. Everybody. And I cannot pretend to know exactly what he had in mind here, but it's a pretty far-reaching word that draws in a wide array of people whom we've probably given up on a long time ago. When we say, "He descended into hell" in the Apostles' Creed, maybe part of what that curious line means is that there is no place that Jesus has given up on—even hell itself.

Jesus utters this line about drawing all people to himself after some Greeks (definite outsiders) arrive at the Passover festival and inquire concerning his whereabouts (John 12:20–21). It's a curious literary device in John's Gospel. People ask Jesus to do various things for almost twelve chapters, and he repeats over and again, "No, can't do that now, my hour has not yet come, my hour isn't quite here yet." The Greeks arrive, the non-Jews, the outsiders show up, and Jesus finally says, "Okay, *now's* the time." And the whole chain of events known as Holy Week is set in motion.

"I will draw all people to myself." Jesus clearly doesn't say *some*. He doesn't say *the faithful* or *those who have obeyed me most*. He doesn't say *those who are righteous and pure as the driven snow*. The word here is *all*. Everybody. And the implication is that the entire cosmos will somehow be drawn to Christ. Somehow, someway, sometime, Jesus says the world will be reconciled to him through his death on a cross: the world's global magnet of love and inclusion.

I've never been able to understand Christian support for state executions. We worship a Lord who hangs on a cross and says things like, "Father, forgive them, they don't know what they're doing" (Luke 23:34). We hear parables in which Jesus's love seems to have no boundaries. And even in passages that seem to imply a divine judgment, it's clearly *God* who is final judge and not human beings. That is the bottom-line source of my opposition: executions cut off any potential possibility of future repentance and change for the guilty.

"I will draw all people to myself." Stop and think about the implications of this verse. It may be among the most radical sayings of Jesus in any Gospel. For some people such radical inclusion is not really good news at all. The words might imply that our behavior on earth *doesn't really count* for anything. And there, in a word, may be the rub (if we're honest) in our overwhelming national support for the death penalty. If God loves all people and will draw all people to himself, then maybe we'd better act quickly and take justice into our own hands and fry infidels *now*, before they get off scot-free in another life.

I once heard a similar line of thinking from a Christian who was responding to the naked universal good news of John 12:32. He became angry. "I've lived right all my life," he said, "gone to church every Sunday, never once cheated on my wife or my income taxes. Pastor, there's *got to be a hell* for those who haven't lived this way!" This is precisely the elder brother's position in the parable of the prodigal son (Luke 15:11–32).

"I will draw all people to myself."

Pastors who preach about the wideness of God's mercy may want to regularly confess that we've got a long way to go in living out the implications of his words. But we cannot pretend we don't know them. We cannot forget that God is final judge and we are not. And we cannot forget that the saving work of the cross is always far more encompassing than any of us can possibly know or fathom.

• • •

In this chapter I have explored five suggestions that truthful preaching might involve on a regular basis: (1) proclamation from the grave (the perspective of truth); (2) the importance of sermonic entry points (setting the stage for truth); (3) learning from poets (the art of telling the truth); (4) truth and theodicy (the reality of a world in which truth is told); and (5) the wideness of God's mercy (the scope of truth telling in the biblical witness).

The chapter began with verses from the book of Hebrews describing a "hope that enters the inner shrine behind the curtain" (6:19–20). Literally, this is the curtain of the law torn asunder by the cross (Matt. 27:51), giving us full access to the God of grace. But I also see a figurative "inner shrine" here—the guarded human heart. Good preaching makes honest gospel forays behind the curtain of our plans and common sin. But preaching alone is not enough. In the next chapter, we'll take a look at the gift and task of pastoral counseling and how clergy are called to peel back the curtain of our excuses and the lies behind which all of us hide so skillfully.

4

Truth and Consequences in Pastoral Care

Daring to Speak the Hard Word

> He reveals deep and hidden things; he knows what is in the darkness, and light dwells with him.
>
> Daniel 2:22

> You know, sometimes I just want to slap certain parishioners, male and female. Why do people sometimes behave so badly?
>
> overheard at a gathering of local clergy

Here's a little pastoral tactic I sometimes use to address a common problem in church life. Feel free to add it to your arsenal too. You might file it under cowardice or deception.

Subject: Checking In

Dear _____,
    I've missed you in worship for the past few months. They taught me in seminary that absence from worship might signal something going on in the life of a parishioner. Are you okay? Do you have any time in the next few weeks to get together and talk? Maybe over lunch? I hope things are going well for you.
    God's peace, Pastor Frank

Actually, I hope things are going horribly for them due to their absence. And I hear you. Call me a coward, and maybe a liar. But perhaps it's better than what I'd really like to say: "Where in the world have you been that's so much more important than worship?"

Our ELCA presiding bishop, Mark Hanson, tells the story of a Lutheran pastor who makes unannounced house calls once per quarter, on Sundays at 11:00 a.m., to various inactive members of his parish. Here's the gist: (Knock on door) . . . "Why pastor, is everything okay? Did somebody die?" "No, I've been worried about you and haven't seen you at the Lord's Table in months. You must be starving spiritually. Can we talk about this?" I love the pastor's response—so full of honesty, care, and candor.

Some information about me you may not want to know: I have only one testicle. Lance Armstrong and I have cancer and a love for bicycles in common, but that's about all. On occasion, my warped friend Ed says, "That takes ball, man." Regardless, I doubt whether I could summon enough courage to knock impromptu on the door of an inactive parishioner and tell him of his spiritual starvation. I'm an introvert and do most of my confronting with a pen or from the safe height of a pulpit that is "six feet above contradiction."[1]

X-ray Vision of the Volcanic Christ

Late at night I've recently been reading an entertaining and very funny memoir by Bill Bryson, one of America's best-loved authors. It's called *The Life and Times of the Thunderbolt Kid*. Bryson was born in Des Moines, Iowa, in 1951. His mom and dad worked at the local newspaper. His father is known as one of the best baseball writers of his era, having covered such events as the famous Bill Mazeroski World Series home run in October of 1960, when the Pirates beat the Yankees in the ninth inning.

There is so much to love about the book, especially if (like me) you were born in the 1950s. Bryson writes about many things that were all the rage for baby boomers, many of which I'd forgotten.

In one section of a chapter titled "Birth of a Superhero," Bryson goes into some detail concerning his childhood fascination with X-ray vision. He (and his lustful adolescent imagination) knew exactly why obtaining such visual superpowers would be interesting. But the whole idea also baffled him. Let me quote a bit:

> I used to give X-ray vision a lot of thought because I couldn't see how it could work. I mean, if you could see through people's clothing, then surely you would also see through their skin and right into their bodies. You would see blood vessels, pulsing organs, food being digested . . . and much else of a gross and undesirable nature.[2]

It's been fun remembering what it was like to be a little boy growing up at a particular time. I'm sharing Bryson's fascination here because Jesus could well be described as somebody with X-ray vision—his laser-like gaze boring into the past of the woman at the well (John 4:1–42), for example, peeling back her excuses and her defenses. She's had five husbands[3] (4:17–18), and the guy she's living with now makes *at least six men*[4] she's been with. How did Jesus know this about her? My heavens, they just met five minutes ago. The scene conjures a possible tabloid cover story: "Shock Messiah Confronts Shady Lady and Serial Marriages at Town Well." Why would Jesus say something so forward and titillating and even downright rude to a relative stranger? But she seems interested in what he has to say. She's attending the equivalent of an inquirers' class there on the public square. I'd be happy with that much interest from a serial monogamist, but Jesus goes straight for the theological jugular.

"Sir, I see that you're a prophet," says this woman. I can think of other words to describe Jesus, this man who just looks right through her. No one else is around. At least this isn't some public spectacle. Like the story of Nicodemus (John 3:1–16), where Jesus is also rather rude, we're listening in on a private conversation, eavesdropping as it were. This private chitchat at the old well is the longest single conversation between Jesus and another person in any of the Gospels—longer than anything he said to his momma or any of the twelve disciples. It's longer than any of Jesus's recorded prayers. This scene at the well was depicted artistically in many ancient church catacombs and, in the early centuries of the church, was a favorite text to prepare catechumens for baptism at Easter.

So I get it, I think. Baptism (the old saving well) washes away sin and shame and all our historic mistakes. But would it *not be enough* for Jesus to offer a generic prayer of forgiveness and absolution? Why get so specific here? Surprisingly, as the story closes, we find this same woman doing handstands in the street, yelling to her neighbors, "Hey, everybody! Gather 'round! Come see a man who told me every single sordid thing I've ever done!" (John 4:29). She seems deliriously happy about this. Do you find this odd? What is going on here? She seems perfectly ecstatic about this man with X-ray vision.

During a common form of Lutheran corporate confession, we address a God "from whom no secrets are hid." Ever think about these words? No secrets. Sometimes during the silence that precedes the actual verbal confession in our liturgy, I'm struck by the power of what's happening at precisely that moment—how all my excuses and facades and masks are stripped away in my own pastoral life. And then it hits me how this is happening *collectively* among us all at the same time. There is perhaps no more honest and truthful moment in anybody's week than the few seconds of silence we share at that precise time. God sees into our lives with X-ray vision. We might all blush if we saw what God was seeing.

But I say thank God for such a moment. Thank God that we worship One who knows us so well, so completely and fully, that even our darkest and most embarrassing moments are brought out into the redeeming and saving light of the Lord. Pastors need to recall this confessional moment later in the week in various encounters (office, lunch, hospital, home visits) with parishioners. Craig Barnes writes:

> Pastors never trust the self-image of anyone. That's because most people construct their identities from an assortment of borrowed images. The typical American today strives to be as attractive as the models on fashion magazine covers, as successful in work as Bill Gates, as sensitive a spouse and parent as Ward and June Cleaver, and as death-defyingly healthy as Lance Armstrong—all while maintaining the inner peace of the Dalai Lama. The fact that these images are often in conflict with each other creates tension within the heart of the individual, who tries desperately to meet all of their demands. . . . The work of Jesus Christ in our lives is to restore [the] divine image, which has become so distorted that it can no longer be recognized. The distortion came

about by our attempts to cram other images into our souls, which made it impossible for us to remember who we were created to be.[5]

It's important (vital, really) to recall that a core purpose of our Sunday gatherings is to give thanks for One who looks into our lives completely and fully, *and still does not look away*. Maybe you're thinking many would prefer a Jesus who only blesses and affirms, soothes and supports. I really don't think so. I'm grateful for a Lord who loves me even in spite of my darkness, confronts the part of me I'd prefer to keep hidden. This woman who met Jesus at the well was dancing in the streets about Jesus's ability to tell her everything she'd ever done. We give thanks for One who knows each of us that completely. Perhaps this is true for pastors in particular whose inner lives often seem like "a bad committee meeting"[6] with lots of competing voices.

Jesus loves and accepts us even in light of the most shameful moments from our past. The man with X-ray vision feeds us all with heavenly food at his table of grace. The converted townspeople said it well so many years ago: "We have heard for ourselves. We know that this is truly the Savior of the world" (John 4:42).

Difficult Confrontation

I've no doubt that pastors can learn a lot from Jesus's caring, confrontational style. But it's also important to recall that *no pastor serves as Jesus*. We are commanded to love "as" Jesus loved (John 13:34), and Luther says the sacrament of baptism makes any Christian a "little Christ." But the diminutive is crucial here. I've made my share of mistakes in this regard over the years, reaching a bit too far to confront perceived waywardness. The following exchange happened pretty much exactly this way in my office one afternoon as I confronted one of our home communion visitors about his absence from the Eucharist on Sunday mornings. It made no sense to me that this person should continue in his role. Admittedly, my history with the man was not the best. Here's the condensed version:

> Me: "I notice you've not been communing with us lately."
> Him: "I just don't feel like it these days. I have a lot of questions about church."
> Me: "Well, I'd be glad to talk about your questions, but you can't take communion to Mabel anymore at the nursing home."
> Him: "Why not? I've developed a very special relationship with her."
> Me: "Because you're not receiving Christ's body and blood with the rest of us flawed sinners on Sunday mornings. And the whole premise for taking home communion to somebody is that you will. You function in this role on behalf of the community, not on behalf of yourself. You're sent from our table to her home. It's not an individual thing between the two of you."
> Him: "You can't take this away from me."
> Me: "Watch me. If you refuse to be part of this community of faith, you can no longer serve in this particular ministry. It makes no theological sense."
> Him: "Well, you'll be seeing me a lot less around here from now on."
> Me: "Less? How could we see you less often than we're already seeing you? Is it possible to attend less frequently than never?"

It doesn't take a rocket scientist to guess that he's been true to his word. I spoke the hard truth that day, but it was hardly spoken in love. I was largely reacting to a negative history that I'd shared with this person. There's a place and time to fire a church volunteer. This one needed to be fired. But I handled the situation poorly. Any X-ray vision I've been given by Jesus could have been used more profitably to explore this person's reasons for being absent. "I have a lot of questions," he said. I missed the opportunity to engage those questions.

This is not to say that difficult confrontation should never occur. Jesus's confrontation at the well is certainly no anomaly. There is a huge expectation (particularly in pastoral counseling) for clergy to be affirming, understanding, loving, and always gracious listeners, nodding and mumbling niceties at all the appropriate times. I once said "bullshit" to our church council on retreat and greatly offended one of our members. I was making a point about the common excuse of being "too busy" to read the Bible. When pressed to explain the offense taken, this very kind and generous man replied, "Jesus would never say that word." There is certainly no textual evidence that Jesus used that exact word, but Ezekiel was forced by God to cook with it (Ezek. 4:9–15), and in Philippians 3:8, Saint Paul clearly used the word to describe what he once valued from his past. The word translated as "rubbish" is *skubala*, which was common parlance for dung. Jesus can be volcanic at times in the Gospels. The common clergy posture of kind, unassuming timidity and unquestioned affirmation of all behavior only serves to warp the real emotive reaction our Savior had to sin and moral rebellion. He was no Caspar Milquetoast in this regard; he regularly leveled disciple and Pharisee alike with stern and serious exchanges.

For example, a bullwhip figures prominently in John 2:15 (mere verses before Jesus's gutsy encounters with Nicodemus and the woman at the well, respectively). A bullwhip! Jarring, isn't it, thinking about our Lord and Savior, that great man of peace, losing it and popping a plump moneychanger on his ample rump right there in the narthex of the temple? A pastor has a lot of spiritual tools at his or her disposal, but

89

I would never resort to a "rawhide mode" of pastoral care if pushed.

My parents took us on a trip once when their three sons were little boys. We went to Maggie Valley's Ghost Town in the Sky in western North Carolina. There we took the chairlift, bought a fake sarsaparilla, and saw cowboys fall from the roof of a saloon in a staged shoot-out. Stoked on the cowboy hormones, we then went across the mountain to nearby Cherokee and got ramped up on the Indians. We begged, pleaded, for bullwhips, and (in a weak moment) mom and dad purchased three. They came to regret that decision.

Anyhow, Jesus made a whip of cords and drove money-changers out of the temple. His disciples recalled that day that somewhere it was written, "Zeal for your house will consume me." (It's written in Psalm 69:9 if you want to examine the context.) Jesus did indeed exhibit zeal that day. The leaders of the temple asked him, "What sign can you show us for doing this?" Rough twenty-first-century translation: "What in the (expletive) do you think you're doing here, Jesus?" Our Lord was indeed consumed with righteous anger. He knocked over tables, scattered coins. He was like Clint Eastwood pushed beyond the boiling point.

It was a nice little financial racket there in the temple—the whole sacrificial animal trade that helped pay for the Roman temple tax imposed by the local government. *Purchase a Pigeon for Passover.* I can see that on a banner out front. Depending on your economic wherewithal, there was something for everyone among the moos and baas and coos. It was a regular business, not unlike the indulgence trade that would emerge in the church many centuries later. This single text has colored an almost universal Lutheran animosity toward fund-raisers of any kind, backed by the feeling that if you're going to give to God, it should be done freely without receiving a sacrificial pigeon or gyro sandwich or whatever.

So Jesus walks into the great city at Passover and just loses it with the bullwhip. Jesus, meek and mild, apparently has limits on his patience. There is a great painting of this scene done by Rembrandt in 1636. You've no doubt seen pictures of Jesus with a halo around his head. Rembrandt chooses to place the halo around *the hands* of our Lord as he swings the whip around.

We don't use the word *docetism* much anymore, but it was a very important word in the first couple centuries of the church, used to describe a popular heresy that Jesus only *seemed* to be human. He looked like a man and talked and walked like a man, but it was all an illusion that masked his complete and total divinity. Human emotions assigned to Jesus were a problem for the docetists. According to them, Jesus loved his earthly mom and dad but never gave them any trouble or back talk. He went to school with the other children but never had a single lustful thought for any girl in his class. He was late for the funeral of his pal Lazarus, but get it out of your head that he actually cried. Maybe Jesus appears angry in this temple scene, but if you look at the original Greek . . . and on and on.

Sometimes it's even hard for pastors, as informed and modern folk, to think of Jesus as a human being who actually had human emotions like sadness, fear, loneliness, and anger. But our creeds struggle mightily to say that Jesus is both divine *and* human. It's tough to wrap our heads around such a notion, but it's very important to try, lest we make Jesus into some divine Superman who commands the impossible when he says, "Follow me."

Jesus gets angry in this old story. Righteously indignant. It's vitally important that pastors see this side of Jesus instead of just the meek and mild Savior who benignly smiles in that famous Sallman Sunday school picture, looking like he's just had a Clairol makeover. It's imperative that we reject our own casual docetism.

Recall the story in John's Gospel that immediately precedes this temple bullwhip scene. Jesus is at the wedding in Cana where he sasses his mother. And he famously turns a great deal of water into many carafes of cabernet. The narrative juxtaposition of these four stories—the water into wine, the cleansing of the temple with a bullwhip, our Lord's brazen honesty with Nicodemus, and then the woman at the well—reminds me that we're dealing with a rather *fermented* Jesus from the get-go. Jesus will bring fizz and pop and challenge into all of our lives, not just affirmation and blessing and *there-there nows*.

As I mentioned earlier, these old stories from John have been used for centuries to scrutinize and prepare adult catechumens readying themselves for baptism at the Great Vigil of Easter. I suspect there are facets of any personality (yours, mine, your best friend's) that annoy and trouble you. And I also suspect that these are the same personality facets and flaws that you and I have been struggling with for many years. What if part of the gospel of Jesus involves not just forgiving those flaws over and again but actually changing us so that we sin a little less? What if the role of Jesus is not just the divine blessing man but also the wielder of the bullwhip, who intends to *drive out* those things that separate us from God? What, in truth, needs to be driven out of our churches today?

Recall that the man who knocked over tables in anger also gathered his disciples in love around a table bearing wine and bread. In the last meal we do indeed find forgiveness and grace. But as Saint Augustine once put it, at this table we also become what we receive—the body of Christ, Jesus in us.

Speaking the Truth in Love

It's easy to expend much negative energy on church issues that don't matter a whole lot. Pastor Tom Marshfield, the fallen cleric in John Updike's *A Month of Sundays*, records in his therapeutic journal an issue from which few clergy have escaped: "Germs and the altar. The sacred chalice versus the disposable paper cup: how many hours of my professional life have been chewed to bitter shreds by this liturgical debate."[7] Most pastors can sympathize with Reverend Marshfield's proclivity to conjure issues that are better left alone.

In relationships involving our direct wisdom, honesty, and courage in pastoral care, how do pastors know when to tell the truth and when to listen compassionately? In their marvelous book on clergy ethics, Walter Wiest and Elwyn Smith offer guidelines for pastors who wish to speak the truth in love in a variety of clergy contexts. Their words are especially helpful for me as I try to decide whether the best tack in pastoral care is support or confrontation:

Truth—which includes both truthfulness and being true—is the key both to ministry and the ethics of ministry. Ministers of the gospel have something to be true to. We have a message to proclaim that is given to us, we do not make it up ourselves, and we are witness to that truth faithfully and with integrity. This is a moral commitment. . . . The truth tells us what we are to be and become. Yet it is more than something spoken or told; this truth is life itself, the new life offered us by God in Christ. This life goes beyond knowing to doing and being. It is embodied by him who said, "I am the Truth." This truth changes us and "trues up" our lives. In and by this truth we live in that mysterious exchange through which Christ abides in us and we in him. This truth makes us free, and very naturally expresses itself in our action. Truth is something we do as well as believe. To be ministers of this truth is to be animated by it, to proclaim what by grace we are. We do what we say.[8]

Wiest and Smith offer a helpful clarification. Truth is not just something we speak. It gives birth to a particular way of life—the way of Christ revealed in Word and sacrament. This way of life will inevitably lead to confrontation with other ways of life.

"Flannery O'Connor," writes Richard Lischer, "has a story about a little girl who loves to visit the convent and the sisters. But every time the nun gives her a hug, the crucifix on Sister's belt gets mashed into the child's face. The gesture of love always leaves a mark."[9] For the balance of this chapter, I want to examine three pastoral care contexts in which speaking the truth in love is vitally necessary for parishioner and clergy health. This arduous and draining work of love may indeed leave a mark on all concerned. Our pastoral motivation in speaking the truth in love should always be clear: we dare to speak not out of personal anger but rather for the benefit and growth of those under our pastoral care.

Truth in Pastoral Visitation

There is a wonderful section in the book of Esther in which the new queen is absolutely conflicted about whether to speak up or shut up. She knows her place as a female outsider in the king's court. Haman (the king's chief adviser) has been behaving badly, and Esther's own people are on the verge of a mini-holocaust. Esther's silence *or* outspokenness may very well seal the fate of her family members. The new queen doesn't know what to do. She's stuck with an important decision and may be wrong no matter what she chooses. Then word comes from Uncle Mordecai, who encourages her to speak the truth: "For if you keep silence at such a time as this, relief and deliverance will rise for the Jews from another quarter, but you and your father's family will perish. Who knows? Perhaps you have come to royal dignity for just such a time as this" (Esther 4:14).

I suspect all pastors can sympathize with Esther's plight. We know that our words, God's Word planted in us, can change everything. It has the power "to pluck up and pull down, to destroy and overthrow, to build and to plant" (Jer. 1:10). With Esther, we know that there will be certain consequences of our choice of words and also probable consequences of our silence. How do we discern when to speak up and when to shut up?

Home Visits

I've always thought that school systems could profitably scrap in-service time and instead allow teachers to visit in the homes of their students. We learn much about people's behavior by their home life and the environs in which they spend much of their waking day. Furnishings, photographs, domestic habits, even refrigerator art reveal much about people that can normally be cloaked and hidden away under their Sunday best. Smart pastors will schedule home visits as a regular part of the workweek, even with people who seem to be healthy and happy. I once heard Gordon Lathrop, the Lutheran liturgics scholar, say in a conference setting, "A pastor doesn't have to knock very hard to find some sort of agony behind every door in the parish." Home visits (much more so than church office encounters) are where people let their hair down and reveal habits that speak volumes.

I was once in the home of a church member who was recovering from outpatient surgery. Although the surgery was the premise for the visit, his main concern was (and always has been) for a son whom I will call Joseph. About thirty-five years old, unemployed, and on disability, he lives at home with his parents. I'd hardly come through the door when a shirtless Joseph burst into the room, revealing a tattoo of a woman's lips kissing his left nipple. Many other etchings covered his colorful torso. "Oh, hi pastor," he grinned, stretching his arms like a cat waking up. "How do you like them? I'm shooting for 60 percent coverage." "Coverage of what?" I asked. "My body," he said. "Too many people conform in this country. I'm not a conformist; never will be." "Yes, I can see that. Tell me something, Joseph." I smiled. "Has it ever occurred to you that *I'm* paying for all your tattoos? That the government you so regularly lampoon is funding the artwork on your body?"

And, in truth, it had not occurred to him. What's the best pastoral approach in such a situation? Ignore the obvious? Applaud Joseph for such a swell set of tattoos? The gentle pastoral jibe invited Joseph to talk about his life in a way that would have never occurred otherwise, certainly not within the confines of a church building. At some point in the future, it will be constructive to talk with Joseph about why he wants such "coverage" and how the scars of Jesus provide the real coverage of peace and strength in the lives of those who choose to follow. Remember the statement from Craig Barnes: "Pastors never trust the self-image of anyone." Joseph's body art is a symptom of a subtext buried deep within. It's doubtful I would ever have seen his tattoos at church.

Hospital Visits

Theresa Sareo, a singer and songwriter, was standing on a New York City street corner when a vehicle plowed into her right leg, eventually resulting in amputation and months of physical therapy. Her trauma surgeon would say that the wound resembled a blast injury, "as if a grenade had gone off in her pocket." Theresa comments, "You just wake up one day with one leg, you're high on morphine, and everyone's who's ever been in your f---ing life is parading by your bed telling you how 'the angels' saved you and everything happens for a reason." She laughs at the diminishment of consolation. "People used to say, 'Oh, once you start writing songs again, I can just imagine.' Oh, can you? Can you? Because I can't. People say the most stupid, small things because they've got nothing better to say."[10]

Eugene Peterson reminds pastors that "the sheer quantity of wreckage around us is appalling"[11]—wrecked bodies, marriages, friendships, alliances, plans, families. How do pastors walk into such wreckage on a daily basis, and what do they say upon arrival? It's easy to become a cynic on the one hand or a theological masseuse on the other, offering clichés and biblical bromide to make the pain go down a little easier. We've all caught ourselves at bedsides mouthing inanities that no one really believes. How does a pastor stay true to Scripture and offer unflinching honesty in the midst of such pervasive wreckage, without sounding like some paid charlatan? There is a huge siren call for pastors to fix whatever's wrong and rush past the wreckage to some brighter day in the future. What pastor hasn't breathed a sigh of relief in walking to the hospital parking lot, knowing that the visit is over for now and he is no longer required to stare death down?

I'm reminded of a scene in David Guterson's novel, *Our Lady of the Forest*, in which a priest nervously offers communion to a young teenager who has been paralyzed in a logging accident. Conversation is difficult for the boy. " 'I don't. Believe in God,' said the boy. 'But go ahead. If you want.' "

> Father Collins performed the Eucharist with an empty heart. The boy's tongue looked dry and pale. His exhaled breath was sour and sweet. The wafer disappeared down his raw red

gullet and his eyes bulged with pain. Father Collins avoided looking at the place where the vent tube penetrated Tom Junior's throat, visible at the sagging lip of his turtleneck. He felt wholly ineffectual. The smell of urine nauseated him. He was frightened and wanted to leave right away. He despised himself and nearly said so. Weren't there priests who worked among lepers, wasn't Christ himself a physician, wasn't he called upon by his very office to salve wounds, anoint the sick, heal, bless, and make hospital visits? Wasn't he called on to look at death, as Mary had looked at her Son's crucifixion? I'm weak, he thought. My soul is weak. You're tired, he said to the paralyzed boy. So I'll leave you now. I'll leave you to rest. And he left with that paltry excuse.[12]

What pastor hasn't felt the discomfort of Father Collins? The problem with such an approach of quick entry and escape is that our primary calling to a ministry of Word and sacrament invites pastors to linger in the mystery of suffering and offer wisdom that seeps into a wound like a good, slow rain. Shared silence (see Job 2:13) is better than quick Hallmark-like pastoral sound bites. There will be times, says Peterson, when we won't feel like doing this ministry and even the church will lure clergy to mouth theological nonsense that goes down easily. However, pastors "are not the minister[s] of our changing desires, or our time-conditioned understanding of our needs, or our secularized hopes for something better. With these vows of ordination we are lashing you fast to the mast of word and sacrament so that you will be unable to respond to the siren voices."[13]

There is a powerful scene in the movie *The Diving Bell and the Butterfly* in which a friend comes to visit Jean-Dominique Bauby, the former editor of *Elle* magazine who is suffering from "locked-in syndrome" after a stroke. He can only blink his eyes to communicate. One blink is yes, two blinks is no. In the movie, the viewer can hear Bauby's thoughts as various visitors (including hasty priests) come and try to offer support. "I pray for you each day," says a friend. "I'm very devout." Only the viewer can hear Bauby's real thoughts in response. The camera looks out through his eyes and we hear, "I want death. . . . I live among a battalion of cripples. . . . Multiple deities have been enrolled to help me." The title of the movie suggests contrasting metaphors in response to such suffering. I must confess that much of my own ministry is an effort to adopt the brightness of the butterfly. I flit in and out rather quickly. Jesus's ministry, in contrast, adopts the diving bell approach.

For example, we tend to approach the story of Jesus weeping over the death of his good pal Lazarus (see John 11) as a "butterfly" sort of story, where good old Jesus swoops in and makes everything right. At first glance, the story appears to resemble a Mighty Mouse cartoon, with Jesus bellowing into the darkness of his friend's tomb, "Here I come to save the day!" But the details of the story don't add up that way. For example, you might ask why Jesus is weeping here. And the initial answer seems to be that he's overcome with grief from the death of his good friend. But a closer look at the text reveals (in v. 33 and again in v. 38) that Jesus is "greatly disturbed." In the Greek, he is "angry" on either side of these tears. So it doesn't make sense that Jesus weeps due to sadness for his good pal. Jesus seems to be weeping because he's completely misunderstood—seen as a man people expect to pull off the next impressive miracle. When he falls short of that they ask, "Well, what's he good for?"

This funeral story, occurring in Bethany (literally, "House of Affliction") and only two miles from Jerusalem (John 11:18), suggests an invitation to linger at the death of Lazarus, not flit by it like a butterfly. In fact, the whole story slowly rubs the reader's face in death time and again in a way that eventually releases us from something even more paralyzing than death itself: our great fear of it.

Agonizing hospital visits in which we walk into the wreckage might be marked beneficially by old stories that slowly probe a subtext much like a diving bell, the story incrementally diving below the surface of things. Such slow unpacking of a biblical story requires pastoral art and timing, of course, certainly something more than nervous flitting that dispenses "butterfly" light at a bedside and nothing more.

Church Office Visits

Very few people initiate office visits to share what a great job their pastor is doing. I'm not complaining about this, but I have learned to listen for the real issue that lurks below the stated one. Normally, there's a problem to share, gripe to discuss, or agony to analyze. There can often be a veneer of cheeriness that precedes the real agenda. I have learned over the years not to hear the compliments I receive as the gospel truth. Praise can be a deceptive cousin to criticism; neither is a consistent indicator by which to evaluate pastoral efficacy. "Woe to you when all speak well of you," says Jesus (Luke 6:26). The young pastor Timothy was told that the church is the "pillar and bulwark of the truth" (1 Tim. 3:15). And there is still some sense that a pastor has been sent to the church to offer an authoritative angle on any word from God. But that authority is eroding. Even with seven years of postcollege theological training under my belt, I've noticed that my opinion is simply one among many opinions. It often carries no more real weight than that of a novice member of church council.

At any rate, church office visits are a good time to instruct people biblically and theologically in a way that might get lost in large committee or board meetings. Regardless of the issue brought to a pastor's office (family discord, congregational conflict, personal problem), our role is to be relentlessly biblical in reframing whatever issue is presented. The privacy (and often leisure) of an office visit provides a fertile context to tell the truth about our place in God's story while speaking openly and in love.

In one of his books, Philip Yancey describes a school of behavior therapy that urges a client to act as if something is true, no matter how strange or impossible such a request might seem. "We change behavior," claims Yancey, "not by delving into the past or by trying to align motives with actions but rather by 'acting as if' the change should happen. It's much easier to act your way into feelings than to feel your way into actions."[14] Yancey goes on to say that such a behavioral construct can be helpful in soured marriages in which the feeling of love has been lost or in relationships in which we have a hard time forgiving another person and cannot imagine the day when the relationship might be mended. Indeed, I recall one marriage that was healed only when I invited the couple to envision that their union was over. Resurrection only works on the dead, after all, and announcing the death of the marriage was the very thing that brought it back to life. We live "as if," then experience spiritual insight.

There is a wonderful scene in one of C. S. Lewis's books about Narnia, *The Silver Chair*. Puddleglum the Marshwiggle is close to being hypnotized by the queen of the underworld, who wants him to believe that Narnia is a land that exists only in his imagination. Puddleglum's monologue is stirring: "Suppose we *have* only dreamed, or made up, all those things—trees and grass and sun and moon and stars and Aslan himself. Suppose we have. Then all I can say is that, in that case, the made-up things seem a good deal more important than the real ones. I'm on Aslan's side even if there

101

isn't any Aslan to lead it. I'm going to live as like a Narnian as I can even if there isn't any Narnia."[15]

Will Willimon asks a very important question that helps me frame most any visit that might occur in the church office: "Who tells us the story of what is happening in the world today?" Oprah? Katie Couric? The bald truth is that most parishioners (and many pastors) are formed by television rather than the Bible, revering Scripture more than actually reading it. Our task in these days of media saturation is often *counter-formation*, offering an alternative story that many Christians have essentially abandoned. So a large goal in any counseling setting is to awaken what Paul Ricouer called "a second naiveté" in approaching and using the biblical text for a culture that tends to equate New Testament parables with nursery rhymes of a cow jumping over the moon. I am "lashed to the mast" of the Bible and need to ask of every visit: why is this person making an appointment with me, a pastor, rather than a secular counselor? Surely the answer is rooted in more than the fact that I offer my services for free.

Daniel's Counseling Style

This chapter opened with a promise from the book of Daniel: "He reveals deep and hidden things; he knows what is in the darkness, and light dwells with him" (2:22). Assuming that God brings light to our darkness, it might behoove a pastor to closely examine Daniel's counseling style in relationship to his central counselees, various royalty formed by a competing narrative. Before getting into the details of Daniel's counseling, I find it fascinating that the prophet is given the name Belteshazzar by the Babylonian palace master (Dan. 1:7). One of Daniel's royal counselees is named Belshazzar (Dan. 5:1). The similarity in names suggests that counselor and counselee (prophet and king) are potentially shaped by the same forces. The pastoral counselor can draw upon the competing true narrative handed down by God but must forever be wary that another false story shapes even the best of us and lurks nearby.

I close this chapter on counseling by highlighting several facets of Daniel's counseling style. Please recall that Daniel resides in a foreign land as these counseling sessions occur. He is the "resident alien" counselor. So are we, in many ways.

When other counselors fail the king, Daniel is summoned (Dan. 4:19–27) to provide interpretation of a bizarre dream, almost as a last resort. The dream initially terrifies our hero. I find great comfort that Daniel at first serves as "pastoral masseur" for the king in Daniel 4:19: "My lord, may the dream be for those who hate you, and its interpretation for your enemies!" Even prophetic counselors can succumb to the temptation of serving as court sycophant. The king has just complimented Daniel in a way that must have felt quite flattering: "You are endowed with a spirit of the holy gods" (4:18). No pastor is immune to the possibility of getting sidetracked by accolades from the powerful.

But Daniel eventually gets around to telling the truth. The king will learn a hard lesson and behave like a beast[16] for seven years, "until you have learned that the Most High has sovereignty over the kingdom of mortals" (4:25). It's an old lesson dating back to Eden: God is king and we are not. The same lesson is repeated again in Daniel 4:32 for the royal counselee who may be slow to understand.

Further truth is spoken to the king in Daniel 4:27—personal righteousness and mercy to the oppressed will be signs that atonement for sin has been accomplished. Prophetic counsel always involves specific change and repentance.

103

The lesson for the king concludes after seven years (sometimes counseling takes this long) with several concrete behaviors: the Most High is blessed (4:34); reason returns (4:36); and praises of truth and justice honor the true "King of heaven" (4:37). Daniel had counseled that the king would not regain true health "until you have learned that the Most High has sovereignty over the kingdom of mortals, and gives it to whom he will" (4:25).

Recognizing Daniel's situation as our own is a key for any pastoral counselor who seeks to speak truth to the false powers that shape nations and their citizens. Effective and truthful counseling will unavoidably deal in confrontation, consequence, and conversion. Like King Belshazzar (Dan. 5:1–30), our alter ego, we have praised "the gods of silver and gold, of bronze, iron, wood, and stone . . . but the God in whose power is [our] very breath, and to whom belong all [our] ways, [we] have not honored" (5:23). Effective pastoral counseling seeks to name the misplaced power and offer an alternative narrative. "We know that we are God's children, and that the whole world lies under the power of the evil one. And we know that the Son of God has come and has given us understanding so that we may know him who is true; and we are in him who is true, in his Son Jesus Christ. He is the true God and eternal life. Little children, keep yourselves from idols" (1 John 5:19–21).

One agonizing task of effective pastoral care is helping parishioners name and own the idols that cause a variety of unhealthy behaviors. Though they may not know it at the time, parishioners come to pastors not just for affirmation and a listening ear. They want to know what we think of their lives within the context of a very old competing narrative, much of which may be long buried. Like it or not, we are called upon to do more than listen. We are called to speak the truth in love. Learning to do so is a lifelong task. Spoken truth will require immense energy and courage and may cause undesirable responses or require explanations. The longer a pastor is on site, the more risks we can venture in this regard. This does not preclude the possibility that new pastors will be called upon to speak truth during the first day on the job, but certainly suggests a recognition that trust is built over time.

In the next chapter, I turn to the importance of catechesis and teaching in pastoral ministry. Speaking to a group is different from speaking directly to an individual. In some respects, we can only become Jeremiah in a public setting after we've served as Nathan in private. Both models are important in church life.

5

Truthful Teaching

The Importance of Creative
Catechesis for Daily Discipleship

Above all, clothe yourselves with love, which binds everything
together in perfect harmony. And let the peace of Christ rule
in your hearts, to which indeed you were called in the one
body. And be thankful. Let the word of Christ dwell in you
richly; teach and admonish one another in all wisdom; and
with gratitude in your hearts sing psalms, hymns and spiritual songs to God.

Colossians 3:14–16

For I want you to know how much I am struggling for you,
and for those in Laodicea, and for all who have not seen me
face to face.

Colossians 2:1

And to the angel of the church in Laodicea write: I know your works; you are neither cold nor hot. I wish that you were either cold or hot. So, because you are lukewarm, and neither cold nor hot, I am about to spit you out of my mouth.

Revelation 3:14–16

One of the greatest weaknesses in our teaching and leadership today is that we spend so much time trying to get people to do things good people are supposed to do, without changing what they really believe.[1]

Dallas Willard

The letter to the Colossians is filled with dozens of imperative verbs. The imperative is often invoked by royalty ("Bow before the throne"), parents ("Take out the garbage and brush your teeth—now"), and other voices of authority ("Get out of the car with your hands up"). Imperative verbs do not beat around the bush. They are rarely ambiguous. Such language hardly ever masks a hidden agenda. Instead, the imperative expects radical obedience, complete submission, and total compliance.

As you might guess, Americans generally do not respond well to imperative directions. We recognize the necessity of certain one-word driving imperatives such as "STOP." But for the most part we are stubborn and rebellious creatures and don't like to be told what to do, even if what we're told to do is best for us. I've always been amused that two of the most common slogans in our country are in direct contradiction with each other: "There ought to be a law against that" and "It's a free country." In America, we prefer words or phrases like *discovery*, *experimentation*, and *figuring things out on our own*. So when Paul rattles off this rather long list of imperatives—clothe, bear with, forgive, teach, admonish, sing, and on and on—I can almost hear a little switch go off for American readers.

107

Paul is addressing a Christian community[2] in a hostile environment, and he's worried sick over these new Christians. Earlier in this letter to the Colossians, he wrote, "I want you to know how much I am struggling for you, and for those in Laodicea" (2:1). Laodicea was a neighboring town just up the road from Colossae, less than ten miles away. Paul is worried about false teaching and halfhearted commitment. The crucified and risen Christ tragically addresses these same Laodiceans several decades later, early in the book of Revelation. Christ says, "I know your works; you are neither cold nor hot. I wish that you were either cold or hot. So, because you are lukewarm, and neither cold nor hot, I am about to spit you out of my mouth" (Rev. 3:14–16). It's not a very polite image, this spitting Jesus. It may be one of the most devastating things our Lord ever said. Jesus apparently prefers a *completely cold* person (that is, someone who has fully rejected him) over someone who occasionally dabbles in the faith. This is a strange idea, but Christ seems to find undeveloped and occasional Christians more distasteful than atheists, agnostics, and others who remain consistently cold to his way of life.

So you can see Paul's urgency and concern. If the neighbors just up the road in Laodicea eventually lapsed into lukewarmness, his worry for the Colossians is well-founded. Paul's long list of imperatives is meant to counter a Christianity that never matures. All these imperative verbs are meant to lead people to a discipleship with depth, to help form us in the faith, to give the Holy Spirit room to work in our lives. They are all wonderful practices capable of leading us closer to Jesus. They describe the behavior and lifestyle of an authentic disciple. "Clothe yourselves with compassion, kindness, humility, meekness, and patience" (Col. 3:12). But there's just one problem. We'd rather dress ourselves, thank you very much. Imperatives make us nervous. He may as well have thrown in, "nail yourself to a cross next Tuesday."

In the Lutheran church today, we have a fairly good idea of what the phrase "justification by grace through faith" means. Salvation is a gift, free of charge; we can never earn it. We have a devil of a time, however, talking about sanctification, holiness, or growth in faith. Perhaps born of our great Reformation heritage and the three *solas*—by faith, word, and grace *alone*—we are nervous about any sort of imperative language. It seems legalistic or conditional. We've got a wonderful theology. But Lutherans do not have an impressive track record in forming disciples who are on fire for Jesus. In fact, we have raised several generations of lukewarm Christians in the Lutheran church. How has this happened?

I'm convinced that one central reason we're lukewarm is that we're unable to talk theologically about sanctification (or holiness or growth in faith) with any real depth. We fear sounding like fundamentalists when we do.[3] We have largely settled for a nonthreatening, lukewarm version of the Spirit. In our model constitution of the ELCA, it has always disturbed me that an active member of the Lutheran church is defined as someone who communes once per year and makes one contribution of record. When our expectations of participation are so low, is it any wonder that we have raised several generations of lukewarm Christians?

If you read Colossians closely, you'll notice that Paul does not begin with the imperative. He first makes several very important indicative observations. Try these on for size: "You were buried with him in baptism, you were also raised with him through faith in the power of God" (2:12). "You have died to the elemental spirits of the universe" (2:20). "You have died, and your life is hidden with Christ in God" (3:3). You were buried. You have died. If this is true—that we have died in baptism—then Paul's imperative list is not some burdensome series of legalisms rubbing us the wrong way. It is spiritual CPR for dead and buried people like us. Compassion, kindness, humility, meekness, and patience are not achievements for us to strive for. They are the very breath of God conveyed to us by the Spirit. Clothe yourselves with these gifts, Paul urges. In the early church, people were baptized in the buff, drenched in the death of Christ, and clothed with a new white garment to symbolize this idea of a new spiritual wardrobe. Then they spat into the darkness, rejecting Satan and all his empty promises. The drama of dying and rising was clear.

Every imperative verb used by Paul to encourage the Colossians should be read in light of people like us who are dead and buried in baptism. Paul's audience has drowned in Jesus and now breaths God's new air. To them he says, "Let the peace of Christ rule in your hearts. . . . Let the word of Christ dwell in you richly. . . . Sing psalms, hymns, and spiritual songs." These are not rules but rather traveling music, directives for the newly born.

How do we recover this ancient baptismal identity as people who have already died and risen—for ourselves, for people who are just learning to know Jesus, and for others who have yet to come but who will be led to our congregations by God?

First, we can no longer assume that whole generations of Christians are learning the faith by osmosis or dumb luck. God has no grandchildren. We have ahead of us a huge challenge of teaching and catechesis and sharing the faith, often to adults who have no Christian history or memory. Meeting the challenge will mean offering a much longer process of discipleship to those inquiring about the faith.[4] We do a disservice to many new Christians by only offering a six-week new member class and a handshake. I suspect our inattention

110

to Christian formation at entry points into the congregation encourages many backdoor losses.

Second, if we die in baptism, if we are "buried with Christ," as Paul puts it in this letter, then our baptismal space should visually convey something of this death. We may need to make changes in our historic worship spaces—not just for the sake of change but to equip the people of God to live out the odd, liberating imperatives breathed into us by the Spirit. In my former parish in Virginia, we built a new font in a cruciform shape—with an upper pool to accommodate infants and a lower (much larger) pool to baptize adults. There was no mistaking the threshold effect such a font conveyed in that worship space. Even in the much older and neo-Gothic space in which I now serve, we moved the font from an almost hidden baptistery to a location more central. We spent a full year in dialogue and study with a planning group and the congregation. That single architectural shift has shaped our understanding of mission powerfully in the last five years. I recall a homeless man who stopped at the font one Sunday morning, unsure of exactly what to do after watching congregants dip their hand and make the sign of the cross. He looked into the water, placed both hands in, and washed his face, coming up from the water glowing with acceptance and the Spirit. The placement of the font has had a leveling effect on all of us in a congregation in which very wealthy people mingle among the penniless.

Third, we must be honest with one another about what membership in the church is and is not. It seems the Rotary Club expects more of its members than the church does. All across America, the mainline church is in danger of becoming the Laodicea of the twenty-first century. We have often perpetuated lukewarmness in the name of inclusivity, always ready to receive others on their terms rather than Jesus's. It is difficult to name our lack of commitment out loud and deal honestly with the false gods of wealth and privilege that woo so many. It's much easier just to serve as the hired chaplain who baptizes, marries, and buries whomever's at hand. But our aim and calling as church is nothing less than this: to assist the Holy Spirit in forming disciples who are so clear in their Christian identity that with Saint Paul we arrive at a similar radical confession: "That whatever we do, in word or deed, we do everything in the name of the Lord Jesus, giving thanks to God the Father through him" (Col. 3:17). Again, entry points into the community of faith are extremely important as we spell out with clear teaching what is expected of new disciples. In some ways, we have returned to challenges similar to those that faced the early church.

Athens, USA

I was walking across the beautiful campus at Virginia Tech not long ago and stopped for a few minutes at one of the many kiosks that encourage students and organizations to post news of events, newly forming groups, musical happenings, and religious services. Reading the flyers made for a fascinating few minutes. I noticed a lot of words ending in the letters *ic*. Organic, karmic, cosmic, ecologic, geopolitic.

Every conceivable group was issuing an invitation. Of course, Virginia Tech is not unusual in this regard. Walk a couple miles across the University of South Carolina campus a couple blocks from the church building where I'm a pastor or into the coffee shops and bars in any city and you'll find the same thing. Each of the flyers makes an urgent appeal to the heart and soul, some sort of claim or premise that could fix your life, solve a problem, or mend the world. The flyers exude more urgency (and clarity) about their various messages than our churches often do.

In Acts 17, Saint Paul is in the ancient city of Athens. He's waiting on his pals, Timothy and Silas, to show up. Paul has a bit of time on his hands, so he just walks around the city and takes in what's there. I have a pastor friend who calls this "Ministry by Walking Around" MBWA for short. He sets out once a week or so from the home base of the church building and talks to whomever he bumps into, just to chat and check the pulse of the neighborhood. I occasionally encourage our own church members to walk a half mile in any direction, stop, and ask a stranger, "Could you tell me how to get to Ebenezer Lutheran Church?" The answers always surprise and instruct us. Many have no idea where the church building is located—even if they're standing two blocks away.

Saint Paul is engaging in a bit of MBWA in the Acts account. He walks around the marketplace of ideas about life and God, which, in its diversity of thought and depth of passion, was much like a citywide version of Virginia Tech's kiosk. Verse 21 gives readers a good picture of what life in Athens at that point in history was like: "The Athenians would spend their time in nothing but telling or hearing something new." Paul engages his own people in the local synagogue, strangers in the marketplace, Epicureans (v. 18) in a restaurant. (They came to be associated with a fondness for fine food but originally believed that everything happened by chance and that if God existed, he was remote. Their motto: eat, drink, and be merry.) Paul also mingles with Stoics, who (in contrast to the Epicureans) believed everything was of God and nothing happened by chance. Taking out the garbage at 9:17 p.m. was ordained. No free will for the Stoic. Swallow your suffering and move on.

In the city of Athens proper, nobody really cared enough about what Paul was saying to get all that heated up about it. His message was one among many posted on the local kiosk of ideas. Athens was a large salad bar of thoughts and philosophies from which to pick and choose.

Like it or not, this is the lay of the land in a new millennium. The church does not have the same moral authority, the same widespread admiration, the same assumed biblical starting point that it did sixty years ago. Perhaps that is a good thing. It has reminded the church of its apostolic beginnings. It has reminded us that we were originally mission-minded people. It has reminded us that Jesus said, "go and make" (Matt. 28:19), *not* "come and sit."

Rather than waiting for people to show up at our beautiful church buildings and moving worship services, which might have worked a half century ago, we are now made to do what we were always called to do: get out of the building and engage people *where they are.* The implication is that we need to find new ways of being church together, which will take time. But church buildings across the Christian spectrum and in cities across the nation are closing because people huddle together in their safe confines of stained glass and wonder why new members aren't showing up anymore.

So Saint Paul walks around the city. He does not wait for people to show up in the synagogue so he can count heads, ciphering an average attendance for somebody back in Jerusalem. That single biblical truth might be enough to help us think in a new way about being the church in the city today.

Paul walks directly into Athens's variety of beliefs and philosophies and urgent ideas. And he engages Athenians about Jesus and the scandal of the resurrection—the raising of a body from the dead. For Greeks, this was the ultimate joke. Please notice the interesting contrast between the numerical response here in Athens and the day of Pentecost in Jerusalem.

In the latter instance, thousands (Acts 2:41) were converted by a single sermon from Peter. Paul's *collective sermon series* in Athens resulted in only two named converts—Dionysius and Damaris (Acts 17:34). Paul will not resort to just anything to win converts, even if he says elsewhere that he's willing to "become all things to all people." He refuses to fall into the culture and be swallowed by it in the name of Jesus.

I mention this because if we are indeed living in the equivalent of first-century Athens, then church growth as we normally measure it may be a little slow. In a new era of faithful evangelism, we may need to let go of counting and focus on real disciple-making. A true coming-to-Jesus will take time. And it may have little to do with numbers.

In order to fully and faithfully engage the city in all its diversity, we don't need hyped-up evangelists who corner people for the kingdom. But we do need people who are conversant about Jesus—why he matters, and why he matters specifically to people who have already signed on as apprentices and disciples. There are a lot of people in a culture such as ours who are "groping for God" (Acts 17:27). But our calling isn't to manipulate them into salvation. Unfortunately, we've got far too many friends of Jesus trying to do just that.

Our calling in engaging the city as Christians is to begin the conversation about Jesus and return to the conversation when we see an opening. It is not our job, after all, to convert somebody. That, ultimately, is the Holy Spirit's work. This old story from Acts attests that Paul "argued" (17:17) with some people about Jesus and "debated" (17:18) with others. Perhaps both evangelical postures have their place. But I don't recommend them in most instances. Argument and debate only create more distance. What the church needs most today are Christians who are so well formed biblically and theologically that they naturally and nonthreateningly engage the city around them with conversation about Jesus. Conversion may or may not follow. This means that a congregation will not only *support* seminaries but will also (in a fashion) *become* one. If the church is to be a place where the baptized are shaped and formed for the ministry of conversation and acts of mercy in the city in Jesus's name, creative catechesis is a key.

One thing about Paul in this slice of Scripture from Acts 17: he was relentless about the gospel. He took it all over town. He listened well to the competing ideas, the philosophers, and the cagey professors. The guy got out. And he took with him Jesus, always Jesus.

God has a love for the city. The city was where most early churches flourished. But today as Christians encounter the city, they tend either to *withdraw* from its inhabitants in holy huddle or to *overwhelm* its inhabitants by aggressive evangelism. We can no longer rely on drawing people to Jesus because of the lovely music or beautiful architecture or staff winsomeness, waiting for people to show up and experience those things. A church's attractive qualities are important, of course, but there are myriad pulls in modern culture that woo the masses far more effectively. "American Christians," claims L. Gregory Jones, "have largely lost a rich familiarity with ruled patterns for reading and embodying Scripture, the kind of familiarity that shapes people's lives and, at its best, enlivens a scriptural imagination."[5] Jones cites the example of how the mainline church's decades-long emphasis on "biblical method" has contributed to our loss of familiarity with Scripture. He quotes a United Methodist bishop, Kenneth Carder, who says, "It is much easier to argue about evolution and creation than it is to live as though this is God's world. Debating whether a 'great fish' really swallowed Jonah is far less costly and risky than acknowledging that God loves our enemies as much as God loves us."[6]

The best kind of ministry in the city in a new millennium may be Ministry by Walking Around—maybe within a half-mile radius—and taking Jesus, always Jesus, with us. If Jones is correct, what sort of courses might smart congregations offer to equip our people for this new walk?

Chatting with an Atheist

> **Chatting with an Atheist (Room 111)**—Author Sam Harris has become one of America's most vocal critics of the church. Class members will read and discuss his bestselling book *Letter to a Christian Nation*. One reviewer has noted, "Harris has consolidated his disdain for religion in a withering attack on Christianity." The *Wall Street Journal* calls the book "a breath of fresh fire." We'll take a close look at Harris's arguments in an effort to be more conversant about our own beliefs with those we may know outside the church. Even though we may not agree with the author, it's good to know what such people are thinking. Especially if we take evangelism seriously. Participants will need to buy their own book either online or locally. Weekly reading will be assigned. Leader: Pastor Honeycutt.

One of the strangest realities in contemporary church life is our silence about Jesus, even with other Christians. And one of the oddest realities in the publishing world is the contemporary atheist's obsession with God and the historical Jesus, even as they've presumably given up on both. Few atheist writers are more winsome and funny than Sam Harris. Even though he often uses unfair caricatures of Christians—constantly and maddeningly employing a straw man person of faith to drive home points with which no sane person could possibly disagree—Harris is worth reading. His short book *Letter to a Christian Nation* reveals his disdain not only for Christianity but for all religions. He argues that belief in God

117

is not only childish but also dangerous. Harris and others like him represent the fastest-growing group relating to religious belief in the country, almost doubling since 1990, "from 8.2% of the population then to 15% today, the largest gain in any group."[7] Let me quote a bit from his introduction:

> Many of us may not care about the fate of civilization. Forty-four percent of the American population is convinced that Jesus will return to judge the living and the dead *sometime in the next fifty years*. According to the most common interpretation of biblical prophecy, Jesus will return only after things have gone terribly awry here on earth. It is, therefore, not an exaggeration to say that if the city of New York were suddenly replaced by a ball of fire, some significant percentage of the American population would see a silver lining in the subsequent mushroom cloud, as it would suggest to them that the best thing that is ever going to happen was about to happen: the return of Christ. It should be blindingly obvious that beliefs of this sort will do little to help us create a durable future for ourselves—socially, economically, environmentally, or geopolitically. Imagine the consequences if any significant component of the U.S. government actually believed that the world was about to end and that its ending would be *glorious*. The fact that nearly half the American population apparently believes this, purely on the basis of religious dogma, should be considered a moral and intellectual emergency.[8]

Those are harsh and true words for the church. I have a good friend who once referred to himself as a Frisbeetarian. He didn't believe in a traditional or metaphysical God but whimsically claimed that his own soul (like a Frisbee) would float up on a roof at the point of death and nobody would be able to get it down. Larry's main problem with Christianity at that time (he still retains healthy qualms) was that Christians seemed to be so insufferably certain about what no one could prove. He'd never been invited to engage Christianity with his mind, even though doing so was certainly mentioned by Jesus as an orthodox way of loving God (Luke 10:27).

A large purpose for the Chatting with an Atheist class was to help class members talk back to Harris in ways that would reveal their beliefs about the Bible and about Jesus—beliefs that perhaps did not match Harris's caricature. Part of each class session was spent in pairs role-playing. One person always played the part of Harris, using his arguments about the Bible and God in particular. The other person in the pair shared her own reasons why the biblical narrative was important and why life with God was a compelling faith stance. There was much to talk about. Harris's writing style is candid and direct, albeit inflammatory at times: "The God of the Bible . . . is not a moderate. Reading Scripture more closely, one does not find reasons to be a religious moderate; one finds reasons to be a proper religious lunatic—to fear the fires of hell, to despise non-believers, to persecute homosexuals, etc. Of course, anyone can cherry-pick Scripture and find reasons to love his neighbor and turn the other cheek."[9] Harris is also guilty of cherry-picking as he indicts the God of the Bible. One positive outcome of the course was that participants were forced to formulate their personal understanding of Holy Scripture—all of it, even the "tales of terror."[10]

In short, the class was (in large part) evangelism practice for Lutherans who are not used to talking about their faith. Ideally it will lead to conversational engagement with others in the public square with the reality of Acts 17 in the background. The class also revealed several realities and ongoing needs: (1) As we engaged Harris's ideas, most agreed that we knew people who were much like him; (2) we agreed that if atheists were taking all of the Bible seriously, Christians should be all the more conversant concerning its contents, even the strange parts; (3) we should stop allowing fringe Christian voices to speak so regularly for the church;[11] and (4) a conventional "Sunday faith" won't be enough to quench the religious thirst of a seeker who may be looking for Jesus in our congregations, perhaps having just left a long period of agnosticism or atheism. To follow Christ means following him into the twists and turns of any given week, which makes us take seriously Luke's invitation to live faithfully "so that you may know the truth concerning the things about which you have been instructed [*catecheo*]" (Luke 1:4). Knowing the truth about Jesus may be a very different enterprise for those who have been instructed and catechized in the faith already.

Tuesdays with Jesus

I know the story of the call of Matthew (Matt. 9:9–26) doesn't actually mention a particular day, but let's pretend it was Tuesday as Jesus sits down for dinner in that house. He's just called Matthew (the notorious IRS man) from his day job. Tuesday it is.

Matthew is at work when Jesus calls him, and the tax man gets up and follows. He's right in the middle of a typical nine-to-five day when Jesus strolls into his life. And nowhere do I see any ecclesiastical caveats like, "Follow me when you have time to follow" or "Follow me on Sunday mornings" or "Follow me at your own convenience" or even "Follow me when you've got me all figured out." No, it's a workday for Matthew. Jesus calls the little tax cheat away from his livelihood (v. 9) and wants him to start living a new way right there and then. Discipleship usurps our jobs; conversion to Christ takes precedent over and recasts our livelihood; money making takes a back seat to following Jesus. Whatever we call gainful employment will now be reshaped and newly envisioned with the gospel clearly in mind. In short, God will not be kept in a convenient box.

Clear on the cost of discipleship, we can throw a little party. The Bible calls it dinner in verse 10, but the time of day is actually ambiguous in the Greek, so let's call it lunch. A Tuesday lunch gathering with Jesus. He's a bit worn out, I'd say, from all his travels, consorting and cavorting with tax collectors, whores, welfare frauds, ex-cons, adulterers, and those with no green cards. The man needs nourishment, right? He's human, say our creeds, so he got hungry and thirsty, weary from all this ministry of crossing the tracks to include people others hated.

Just when Jesus says "pass the peas" at lunch that Tuesday, some church council people and their pastors, an outraged entourage from a local congregation, burst through the door and demand to know what in the world Jesus thinks he is doing. They actually corner his followers and lividly inquire whether or not Jesus has any sense of propriety at all. Does he have any idea who he's buttering his bread with?

And right there (I've always loved this about Jesus) the man taps a water glass with a spoon and delivers a zinger of a sermon about mercy and love and healing and how the self-righteous can just go to hell. It was quite a homily, and I'd say it silenced the lunchroom interlopers, who exit huffily to now talk about the man in the parking lot. "Pass the biscuits, please," says Jesus.

But no. Just before the next bite, some disciples of John barge in (v. 14), and they have a question about fasting. "God says we're supposed to sacrifice and look forlorn when thinking about divine things and here you are stuffing your face all the time, Jesus. What's up with that?"

121

And so our Lord, with no hint of annoyance that the mashed potatoes are getting cold, delivers a second little homily to a completely different audience and says something about new wine and old wineskins and how mixing the two will leave you with fermented grape juice exploding in your face. His questioners look at one another, a bit flummoxed by this vexing tale from the vineyard.

I absolutely love verse 18. "While he was saying these things to them . . ." That is, smack dab in the middle of that second sermon to that second group of lunch interrupters, a leader of the synagogue bursts in and kneels before Jesus. Try to imagine this all happening at Cracker Barrel. This man interrupts those *other* interlopers who, in turn, had also intruded uninvited to interrupt *another* set of unexpected questioners. Are you with me here? It's the same meal. Two sermons have been offered and now this. I'd say the side dishes are a bit tepid by now.

So this poor man, a father in a puddle of woe, throws himself on Jesus and says, "My daughter is dead, but I know she'll be okay if you just come. Please come." And so Jesus, God bless him, gets up right then and there with the napkin still under his chin and heads down the road with this grieving daddy, leaving the astonished lunchroom guests with mouths agape and more than a few leftovers.

I generally clear the calendar for funerals. There's something about a dead person that demands your full and immediate attention. Death is a big deal. Jesus, surely, will make a beeline for this little girl's bedside and do his thing. *But wait.* Not so fast, Jesus. On the way from that lunch filled with various interruptions, a final interrupter on this one Tuesday in the life of Jesus pops out of the crowd and reaches out for the man (v. 20). "Maybe if I just touch him," she thinks. "I don't need much, just the fringe of his shirt." But Jesus gives her a lot more than that, doesn't he? He stops. He chats and heals. Please ponder this. After all the other shifts and changes in this one day, enough interruptions for a year of Tuesdays, Jesus stops on his way to a funeral and tenderly encounters this needy woman who's been bleeding for twelve long years. It's just too much to take in.

And I know what I would have probably said. Something like, "Woman, do you have *any idea* what kind of day I'm having here? Take a number, will you?" But remarkably, unbelievably, our Lord stops and kindly offers a touch and a word before proceeding on to the bedside of that little girl. Have you been counting? This is the fourth interruption in a scene that began with a simple bite of lunch. What does this story tell us about Jesus anyway? And more to the point, about his disciples? Or about people like Sam Harris who've given up on discipleship?

Notice verse 26 of this story: "The report of this spread throughout that district." The report of *what* exactly? News of that little girl running and jumping again? The miraculous is always something of a head-turner.

But maybe "the report" on Jesus also included the various twists and turns and interruptions and calm clarity of the man when he seemed on the verge of being pecked to death by a gaggle of ducks. "Why this, Jesus?" "Why that?" "Why them?" "Please do this for me, Jesus."

He handled it all with honesty, grace, and aplomb. If you're looking for miracles from this particular Tuesday, please don't overlook that one. Some wise person, reflecting on how churches sometimes spend far too much time thinking about how to plan for ministry, how to strategize for ministry, countered that ministry is not something you "go and do" in neat little time blocks. It's something you do *as you go.*

Ministry is the whole day, in other words. Your whole life of days. Here's a little Bible tip for serious readers of Scripture: you might want to keep your eyes on Jesus whenever he happens to sit down for a meal in the Gospels. Chances are, something explosive and powerful and downright odd is about to happen when our Lord eats with his disciples.

So watch this odd man. He's in our lives for a meal of grace. He's guiding, teaching, and leading us to new places with new wine, forever changing the way we look at Tuesdays— and all the days we're given—even giving us courage to die with him.

6

Death and Deceit

The Funeral Service and Holy Truth Telling

We are afflicted in every way, but not crushed; perplexed, but not driven to despair; persecuted, but not forsaken; struck down, but not destroyed; always carrying in the body the death of Jesus, so that the life of Jesus may also be made visible in our bodies.

2 Corinthians 4:8–10

One death is a tragedy; a million deaths is a statistic.[1]

Josef Stalin

In order to know a community, one must observe the style of its funerals and know what manner of men they bury with most ceremony.[2]

Mark Twain

125

Prayer in Jesus' name is noted for his demand that we pray for our enemies, not our illnesses. I've recently heard prayers about radical mastectomies, testicular tumors and sprained index fingers but can't tell you when I've heard a really good intercession for Osama bin Laden.[3]

William H. Willimon

In one of his books, astronomer Chet Raymo describes a collision he witnessed one November afternoon between a skateboarder and a little girl in busy Boston Common. The impact caused the child to be thrown high into the air and fall to the pavement, an accident from which she would fully recover. Raymo reports that it "happened in perfect silence."

What intrigues me about this incident is the author's subsequent reflection upon the child suspended in midair.

During the time the child was in the air, the spinning Earth carried her half a mile to the east. The motion of the Earth about the sun carried her back again forty miles westward. The drift of the solar system among the stars of the Milky Way bore her silently twenty miles toward the star Vega. The turning pinwheel of the Milky Way Galaxy carried her 300 miles in a great circle about the galactic center. After that huge flight through space she hit the ground and bounced like a rubber ball.[4]

Physics and astronomy have drawn my late-night reading attention recently, perhaps because I'm looking forward to the upcoming Perseid meteor showers in early August. Thirty years ago some friends and I hiked up Looking Glass Mountain in North Carolina after midnight to watch the show from the smooth rock face on a clear, moonless evening. We were treated to hundreds of shooting stars. Each August since brings God's curious question posed to Adam and Eve in the garden—"Where are you?" (Gen. 3:9)—more sharply into focus. God is not asking out of ignorance. God certainly knows their cloaked geographical location, just as God knows that I live in central South Carolina and hide as adeptly as our garden-dwelling forebears. The question invites us to ponder our existence, our sin, our time and place in this vast uncharted cosmos, and the improbable notion of a God who knows each of us personally, even by name. *Where are you?* It's a lot to think about. Six billion people on the planet and God knows each of our names and situations. Factor in the reality that multiple galaxies exist for each person on earth and the question becomes even more befuddling. Where am I, indeed? Answering God's question requires perspective.

I recently visited one of our older members, Nola, who will soon turn ninety-eight. Her laugh and smile never fail to pull me out of any pastoral funk. Nola was a tomboy in her youth, and her mother usually called her Dick. A retired nurse and unabashedly scatological in speech, Nola smiles and says, giggling, "Every family needs a Dick." On this visit, Nola describes her lifelong fascination with doodlebugs and how she would insert a piece of thin grass into a long hole to fish for and catch them. "You'd wait for that little piece of grass to wiggle just a bit and then pull out an angry doodler with pincers. I used to fish for doodlebugs for hours." Nola prays for an hour each morning on her knees, with a prayer list that would put any pastor to shame. "In church when I was little, we never looked around to see who was behind us. My momma always told us that we were supposed to focus on God. Sometimes I slipped up and she'd say, 'Now Dick, didn't I tell you not to turn around? Now you say a little prayer asking God to get your heart right.'"

Nola has perspective—the ability to see God in the proximity of a doodlebug and the vastness of the stars. She makes the sign of the cross each day over her body, "always carrying with her the death of Jesus" so that his life may be clearly seen in hers. She has no fear of death; she has crossed over on this side of the grave. "Give ear to my words, O LORD; give heed to my sighing" (Ps. 5:1). Any sighing from Nola is made plain in prayer, releasing her to live joyfully for the better part of a century. How does the church form and shape people who carry the life of Jesus even in the midst of death?

The Reality of Death

For all you young people under the age of forty, here are three little snapshots of life after the half-century mark. The first comes from Steve Martin, the actor, and tells about reading the fine print of a prescription. The excerpt is from "Side Effects," a piece he wrote in 1998.

> This drug may cause joint pain, nausea, head-ache, or short-ness of breath. You may also experience muscle aches, rapid heartbeat, and ringing in the ears. If you feel faint, call your doctor. Under no circumstances eat yak. . . . You may find yourselves becoming lost or vague. . . . This drug may cause visions of the Virgin Mary to appear in treetops. If this happens, open a souvenir shop.[5]

I recommend reading the entire piece to any Christian who takes getting old too seriously. Here's the second portrait of the aging process. It's from an email written by an old Virginian friend named Lowry, who edited the town paper where I lived for many years.

> I think it's time for me to be put away. I went to Kroger's this morning to buy a few things. I had only a hundred dollar bill, and this irritated the cashier ladyperson who had to hunt up change while the line halted. When she returned with the bills I stuck them in one coat pocket and stuck my wallet in the other coat pocket to let the line move on. Outside I stuck two quarters into the newspaper machine.

While I was trying to extract a newspaper without having to set my groceries down, the machine door slammed shut and caught a sizeable piece of my coat in its jaws. I was totally trapped, so I searched for two more quarters with which to make that door open. I didn't have any more quarters. I was trying to wiggle out of the coat under the wondering gaze of several bemused shoppers when one little old man stepped forward with two quarters and freed me. My day has been ruined.

When I lived in Virginia, I always tried to talk to Lowry when I was having an especially bad day at church. His humor was buoying. Find some amusing people in your life to help you cultivate a healthy perspective. Lighten up a bit. And quit worrying so much about your hair falling out.

Here's the third portrait about death and getting older. Maybe you'll recognize this one.

> Jesus himself stood among them and said to them, "Peace be with you." They were startled and terrified, and thought they were seeing a ghost. He said to them, "Why are you frightened, and why do doubts arise in your hearts? Look at my hands and my feet; see that it is I myself. Touch me and see; for a ghost does not have flesh and bones as you see that I have. (Luke 24:36–39)

After his crucifixion, Jesus seems to spend an awful lot of time trying to convince people that he's not a ghost. The disciples are scared out of their wits, and Jesus does all he can to calm them, but I'm not sure it works so well. "A ghost doesn't have flesh and bones. Come on, touch me. Let your fingers do the walking." Would you have gone first? The Bible reports the marvelous fact that "in their joy [the disciples] were disbelieving" (Luke 24:41). I love that line. Joyful agnosticism. Skeptical delirium. Isn't it nice to know that these disciples—the first guys who saw Jesus up and walking around—were just as confused and frightened and worried about dying as we are?

The disciples still think they're seeing a ghost, some apparition (a dream sequence, maybe), so Jesus says, "Now look here. It's me. You guys got anything here to eat? You must have something here. I've seen how you guys can put it away." Everyone knows that ghosts don't eat food. So our Lord munches on a platter of broiled sea bass to prove he's no cousin to Casper. Eats the whole plate right in front of them.

Do you think about dying very much? What that will be like? When it will come? Pastors think about it more and more as the years pass, as they preside over funerals where friends and family are put in the ground, or in little boxes, or scattered on the waters or in the hills. "Ashes to ashes" and all that. But I suspect even pastors think about death silently. It's unavoidable to ponder it as we age. But we sometimes assign a special power to death that's curious given the fact we're Christians. "I believe in the resurrection of the body," we say. But do we really believe that old creedal line?

In eighteenth-century England, it was all the rage to bury people with a fully equipped casket rigged with a string. The string was connected from inside the casket to a bell above ground. You see where this is going. If you found yourself buried alive—it didn't happen often, but once or twice can create panic—then you could pull the string and the little bell would sound. "We've got a live one. Call the backhoe guy." I've seen bizarre pictures of these caskets, fully equipped with every amenity imaginable and, of course, the little bell and sturdy string. It's where we get the expression *saved by the bell*.

It's been well documented that in this country we spend most of our health care dollars on untreatable illnesses that afflict people who are simply getting older. We make choices that suggest a belief that death will never come, where there's always a string to pull, a bell to ring. Our hearts beat 3,153,600,000 times[6] (or thereabouts) over the course of a lifetime. Given the longevity and regularity of the heart, it's hard to come to terms with the fact that the organ will stop beating one day. In one of his books, the late Richard John Neuhaus writes, "The Victorians of the 19th century talked incessantly about death but were silent about sex, whereas today we talk incessantly about sex and are silent about death."[7]

This is not the Christian way, am I right? We've got *good news* about death. "Why are you so frightened?" says the Lord who lives. "Why do doubts arise in your hearts?" Well, we know why—we know all too well. The jocular diagnosis of a trusted physician turns rather dark. Friends die far too young. The evening news reports calamity over the next horizon.

Jesus never said this, but I suspect he might today: "Why do you obsess over pills and doctor appointments and going to the hospital and yet spend so little time in prayer with me? Are you my disciple or not? Why have you chosen to follow these other things so obsessively?"

If you hear all this as some wacky invitation to forgo medical treatment, then you've heard me wrong. God bless all doctors and the marvels of modern medicine. I do think, however, that our trust and hope are misplaced when we look to medicine to solve aging. Especially given the people we claim to be. Why have we so quickly replaced the Great Physician with another temple of healing before which we all bow?

"Why are you so afraid? Touch me. Touch me and see that I'm not a ghost—some figment from the past, from your imagination. I'm alive. Touch me."

131

● ● ●

I went to a funeral recently in the beautiful countryside near Pomaria, South Carolina. It was a gorgeous day—little Saint Matthew's Lutheran was packed, wonderful hymn singing, a powerful sermon from Pastor Mark, a haunting medley of old gospel tunes played impeccably by a master strummer. I was there because of the death of my good friend's father. The tone of the funeral was just right. For a moment, time seemed to hang in the air, and it was like we were all in heaven together—singing, praying, meeting our loved ones again.

At the end of the service, a poem was read. It was written by my friend Melissa. She wrote it just hours after her father died, in tribute to her dad.

> The blossoming things are rambling
> all along this earth,
> but you ramble through my mind,
>
> your frame no longer thin and frail,
> but robust, full of vigor and life.
> How I want to embrace you once, once more,
>
> but it will not be—
> not in this place, but perhaps there,
> where we will sit and share a meal,
>
> on another holy hill,
> where we will both be at home again
> among the flowers wild
>
> and where all the death
> that threatens us will be tame,
> nothing at all.[8]

The Author of life. That's what Acts 3:15 calls Jesus. "Why are you frightened?" he once asked. We know why.

"So touch me. Touch me and see," he says. "For a ghost does not have flesh and bones as you see that I have."

Ten Tasks

How can pastors bring hope and comfort at funerals and also tell the truth absolutely free from any of the schmaltz or theological hoodwinking that seems to infect so many funeral sermons? I suspect that in the early months of a pastor's tenure in a new call, it's the funeral service, more than any other pastoral act, that establishes clergy authenticity among the gathered people of God. The advent of shared hope and communal trust between pastor and congregation does not happen overnight. And most people are pretty good at silently sniffing out a fraud. So here's some advice:

> Don't make promises God doesn't keep. Account for the shaky ground and patches of quicksand. Don't deny our disappointments or turn away from our broken hearts. Explain the beasts lying in wait, the damaged goods that can't be fixed, the trouble in the streets. Show us God in the horrors hidden under cover of night and the prayers that don't get answered. Make your words equal to our predicament. Give us faith as wild as the world. Describe that and we'll hang on every word.[9]

In that spirit, I offer ten tasks necessary to cultivate a climate in congregations that will help the community and its leaders think truthfully about death and planning for funerals.

1. *Be regularly honest and even playful about your own pastoral mortality.* While shaving one morning I had a brainstorm and rushed for my journal to jot down a note. Anne Lamott, in her book *Bird by Bird*, says that inspiration needs to be recorded when and as it occurs. That done, I realized

my comb was missing. I went from room to room in my underwear, late for an appointment and cursing colorfully, before finally looking in the mirror. Staring back at me was some guy with a comb lodged securely in the hair on top of his head.

2. *Practice biblical restraint in describing a realm we cannot know in full.* One of our church members, Howard, is a funeral home director. We regularly travel to cemeteries in the lead car and have a little time together. Our conversation covers the waterfront, but he has come to expect this invitation: "Howard, tell me an interesting story that has occurred in your line of work recently." I recommend this learning and listening time for all pastors who want to gather wisdom from those who think about death a lot. Howard never fails to come through. He once told me of a dove that was released at a funeral. The dove was supposed to represent peace and love, tranquility and eternity. The bird made one swoop around the cemetery and then another. Just as the bird was heading for the horizon, a hawk descended silently from the trees, grabbed the startled bird of peace in its talons, and flew away for a late lunch. Howard told me of the audible gasps from the startled mourners and shared the words of a colleague, who whispered, "Well, we're never doing *that* again."

In any event, one of Howard's pet peeves is that pastors claim to know more about the next life than the Bible ever attempts to offer. Howard wisely calls for pastoral restraint instead of guessing about things we cannot possibly know. If truth were told, most of us practice a rather Gnostic understanding of the immortality of the soul at funerals. "It's just her old shell she's sloughed off."[10] The word *just* is revealing here. "Your daddy's with Jesus now in heaven, awaiting the great reunion we'll all have as family there one fine day." These well-intentioned statements probably reveal the preacher's uneasiness with a dead body, his rush to find resolution nowhere present in the Bible. Advice from a grieving father: "Don't say it's not really so bad. Because it is. Death is awful, demonic. If you think your task as comforter is to tell me that really, all things considered, it's not so bad, you do not sit with me in my grief but place yourself off in the distance away from me. Over there, you are of no help. . . . To comfort me, you have to come close. Come sit beside me on my mourning bench."[11]

Whether we agree with the old doctrine or not, the Apostles' Creed assumes a resurrection of *the body*,[12] not a resurrection of some ephemeral spirit who dances on the beach in heavenly bliss at the exact point of death. According to this doctrine, body and soul both kick the bucket together when we breathe our last. I've never interviewed a resurrected person and cannot vouch with certainty for this creedal affirmation, but that's the tradition we're passing on. We should at least acknowledge the claim, relying on the Bible for sermonic text rather than our own best guess —which often serves to mask our discomfort with death.

3. *Use the whole Bible, and not just funeral favorites, at funerals.* Lutheran pastors are quite fond of quoting favorite verses from John 14 and Romans 8 at funerals. Perhaps three-quarters of all funerals I've ever attended use these two passages: (1) "In my Father's house there are many dwelling places" (John 14:2); and (2) "For I am convinced that neither death, nor life, nor angels, nor rulers, nor things present, nor things to come, nor powers, nor height, nor depth, nor anything else in all creation will be able to separate us from the love of God in Christ Jesus" (Rom. 8:38–39). I love these two passages, but please, enough is enough. We tend to omit the voiced honesty surrounding either passage anyway. From Thomas: "Lord, we have no idea where you're going or what

you're talking about" (John 14:5). From Paul: "For your sake we are being killed all day long" (Rom. 8:36, quoting Ps. 44:22).

Many people attending funerals are not church people at all. I sometimes wonder if they leave funerals wondering if the Bible is comprised of two key verses. "Simple, nothing to this book really. It could fit on a matchbook cover. Who needs church to understand that?" No wonder the Barnes & Noble religious section is littered with titles such as *God's Little Devotional Book for Busy Couples*. There is nothing "little" about the Bible. Pastors should access the whole biblical corpus when preparing for a funeral. Otherwise we are wasting a catechetical and evangelical opportunity by recycling the same message over and over. It may be a compelling message, but we can do better.

4. *Decide on one controlling metaphor that links the life of the deceased to all selected Scripture passages.* Recently one of the saints of our congregation, George, died after many years of faithful service as a councilman and lay leader. He was the epitome of what we used to call a "churchman." Always ready with historical context, a witty retort, and a sly grin with sparkling eyes, George grew up on a farm that spanned land connecting two local rivers, the Broad and the Saluda, and he had favorite fishing holes in each. One of my favorite George stories is of him as a little boy running back and forth over that land, between rivers, searching for the biting fish. George did not become a great disciple of Christ by luck but through his love of Jesus revealed in the baptized life. He was a great supporter in the relocation of our old baptismal font to a more central and visible spot in the chancel. His voice could sway many.

All the passages for the funeral service (and all the hymns) served the controlling metaphor of rivers, healing water, and

George's great fondness for the sacrament of holy baptism: Ezekiel 47:9 ("everything will live where the river goes"); Psalm 46:4 ("There is a river whose streams make glad the city of God"); and Revelation 22:1 ("the river of the water of life . . . flowing from the throne of God and of the Lamb"). Here's an excerpt from my funeral homily that evening:

> Tonight's dream-like story from Ezekiel is about an old river that begins as a trickle in the center of the temple, the house of the Lord, and eventually becomes so swift and deep that nobody can cross it. I think George had a very real sense of life beginning at a font such as this one—the water bubbling over stone's edge and flowing down the aisle and getting our socks a little damp and crinkling the pages of our new worship books and out the church door and into the city for the healing and health of all people. "Mortal, have you seen this?" God asks Ezekial. And indeed I think George Caughman did see a very similar vision. He saw the restorative and liberating power of this water. Life begins in the water, begins here at the source, and "everything will live where the river goes."

In many cases, mourners won't remember much from a funeral service. If possible, always provide a tape of the service or a sermon manuscript for later reference. In any case, a controlling metaphor—a single image that is repeated several times and in several ways—is usually enough to carry the gospel into grief's deep confusion. This is the power of poetry as it plumbs the depth of shared experience of God and God's activity with the deceased. A controlling metaphor will awaken other images and memories from all who knew the beloved person and all who know Christ.

5. *Speak of Jesus and his approach to death; avoid the trap of the eulogy.* The passion according to Saint John finds Jesus in a familiar face-off with Pontius Pilate, the man who thinks he has the power to set Jesus free. Pilate asks Jesus a

very straightforward question on Good Friday: *"Where are you from?"* (John 19:9). Jesus could've told Pilate about his own colorful family tree (see Matt. 1:1–17 for a few surprises), but he chooses not to do that. "Where are you from?" asks Pilate. And Jesus says not a word.

We know the answer to that question. Jesus has already answered Pilate once. "My kingdom is not from this world. If my kingdom were from this world, my followers would be fighting. But as it is, well, I'm not from here" (John 18:36). Pilate, as you may recall, got a little huffy with that first answer. By the time Jesus's final sentencing rolls around, Pilate isn't so much put out with Jesus. Instead, he's downright afraid of him. The text says "more afraid than ever" (John 19:8). So Pilate returns to his headquarters in the middle of the night and locates Jesus once more. *Now where'd you say you were from?* Pilate is as nervous as a caged cat.

Notice in John's Gospel how downright calm Jesus seems to be as he faces his execution. After sassing the high priest, he's as cool as a cucumber when a policeman slaps him so hard you can hear the echo (John 18:22). In John's telling, Jesus never once questions his purpose or has even a hint of internal anxiety about his mission. You won't find the words "my God, my God, why have you forsaken me?" (Mark 15:34) in this story. In the other three Gospels, somebody carries Jesus's cross for him. In John, Jesus himself lifts the lumber. Even though the authorities eventually kill him, Jesus still seems to be completely in control of the proceedings.

When the soldiers come to arrest him in the garden, he never once resists. "When Jesus said to them, 'I am he,' they stepped back and fell to the ground" (John 18:6). In the Greek he actually says, "I am" to the soldiers—the divine name from Exodus, the name revealed to Moses at the burning bush, is found here on the lips of Jesus. "I am," he says to the powers that arrive with darkness. And the soldiers hit the deck. It's interesting to contrast this event with a later one, when someone asks Peter if he also is a follower and he answers, "I am not" (John 18:25).

The powers that the soldiers represent do indeed execute Jesus eventually. But please note: they are never in control. The one hanging on the cross, in apparent weakness, is paradoxically in charge. Pilate asks, "Now where'd you say you were from?" He's "more afraid than ever."

Now we the tellers of this story, we the insiders who are aware of the outcome, know exactly where Jesus is from. He's from a kingdom that makes Pilate's domain look like adult bullies playing with tinker toys. Pilate and his cronies have no power over Jesus, and we know exactly why. His kingdom is not of this world. Nobody can touch Jesus. Not even the most well-managed evil, the most heinous suffering, the most brutal jabs and taunts in the world. "Where are you from?" Pilate asks. And we know the answer to that question that makes Mr. High and Mighty Muckety-Muck, the model of decorum and control, so nervous. See who's sweating? Not Jesus. Never once is he out of control in this story. He knows where he's from, knows who his real daddy is. Jesus is in handcuffs before Pilate, but who has the real power?

It is important at funerals to make a case that the deceased also has a homeland other than a particular flag and nation from which decisions and a life flowed. It's easy to spend sermon time eulogizing the deceased, listing accomplishments easily read in the newspaper obituary, accomplishments that seem to have no real connection to Jesus. Paul wrote, "I want to know Christ and the power of his resurrection and the sharing of his sufferings by becoming like him in his death" (Phil. 3:10). It behooves a follower to learn how Jesus faced death. And a believer's funeral service should always reveal more about Jesus and what the deceased knew about our Lord that helped shape his or her life. Our real homeland, our true citizenship, should never be obscured.

6. *Invite parishioners to plan their own funeral.* "One pastor of my acquaintance," notes author Rodney Clapp, "includes an interesting exercise in premarital counseling. She has the couple plan each other's funeral. She finds that this makes the spouses-to-be think about what kind of person their lover may be years or decades later. And then the two start talking about how they might best take care of each other and their marriage right now. By asking how their marriage may end, they discover how it may best begin and be sustained to its end."[13] Pastors might offer a course on death and dying annually (this is consistently the best attended class I teach in any calendar year) that culminates with an invitation to think about one's own funeral service—Scripture passages, hymns, special themes. Saving these reflections in a pastoral file is a great gift not only to the family at the time of death but also to the preacher who is saved from foraging for "funeral homily fodder" in a suddenly very compressed week.

7. *Recall throughout the church year that Christians have "already died."* One of the gifts of the church year from Advent through Christ the King Sunday is that our noses, so to speak, are so consistently and cyclically rubbed in the reality of death that we are freed from its paralyzing power. Fiction writer Ron Rash describes a drowning in one of his novels. The victim is a twelve-year-old girl who falls into an upstate river on Easter break with her family and gets trapped in a river hydraulic. Rash describes the final moments of this little girl's life:

> She remembers her sixth-grade science class, the gurgle of the aquarium at the back of the room that morning the teacher held a prism out the window so it might fill with color, and

she has a final beautiful thought—that she is now inside that prism and knows something even the teacher does not know, that the prism's colors are voices, voices that swirl around her head like a crown, and at that moment her arms and legs she did not even know were flailing cease and she becomes part of the river.[14]

Without explicitly using the word baptism in this passage, Rash evokes the sacramental drowning of any Christian who now becomes part of a long river of voices known as the communion of saints.

I participated in an exercise recently in which the class was asked to list various images that came to mind when they heard the word *baptism*. We came up with a pretty impressive list: *new life, rebirth, cleansing, forgiveness, family, light, refreshment, repentance, creation, body of Christ*. All these are valid and biblical. But nobody came up with the word *death*. Few have in the many times I've participated in this exercise.

But death is a central metaphor for baptism throughout the New Testament. In fact, it may be used more often than any of the words just listed. Saint Paul's famous question from Romans (fondly quoted by Luther in his *Small Catechism* in 1529) is no anomaly: "Don't you know that all of us who have been baptized into Christ Jesus have been baptized into his death?" (6:3). The words *death* or *dying* (or their close cousins) are used fourteen times in the section (6:1–11). "You have died," Paul says in Colossians 3:3. "It's no longer I who am alive," reports the letter to the Galatians, "but Christ who now lives within me" (2:20).

Baptism is a death. Elaborate sermons on dying in baptism were once preached in the early church. The Red Sea story in Exodus, read annually at the Great Easter Vigil, became symbolic of how baptism drowns sin and the old life in Egypt,

141

washing up a new people on the far shore of a whole new land. At one time in church history, a favorite shape for baptismal fonts was the shape of a tomb. Luther himself preferred full immersion in the waters of the font to suggest a visual dying and rising with Christ.

Our actions during a Lutheran infant baptism underscore our reticence to connect it to the metaphor of death. We have a hard time believing babies are sinners from the get-go of human existence. Their perceived innocence clouds our thinking. And so very often the sacrament becomes more about family tradition, flashbulbs, and some fuzzy idea of eternal fire insurance. It's hard to talk about death while holding a beautiful baby. And often in modern Lutheran baptisms (as in the baptisms of many other churches), so precious little water is used that it has been said that our sacrament is more of a dry cleaning.

In C. S. Lewis's book *The Voyage of the Dawn Treader*, there is a selfish and obnoxious child named Eustace. Nobody likes this kid—for good reason. He steals water during a water shortage and generally looks out for nobody but himself. At one point, Eustace becomes so ornery and self-centered that he turns into a dragon and grows scales. Eustace tries three times to scratch off the scaly skin, but each time it grows back. Aslan the Lion (the Christ figure in Lewis's stories) appears and says, "You will have to let me undress you." Think about the baptismal implications of that line. We cannot fix what's wrong with our lives by ourselves. Christ has to undress and drown us. Eustace describes what happens next:

> The very first tear he made was so deep that I thought it had gone right to my heart. And when he began pulling the skin off, it hurt worse than anything I've ever felt. . . . Then he caught hold of me and threw me into the water. It smarted like anything but only for a moment. After that it became

142

delicious and as soon as I started swimming and splashing I found that all the pain had gone from my arm. And then I saw why. I'd turned into a boy again.[15]

In baptism, no matter who we are, or how old we are, or how innocent we appear to be, we are given a new identity. We receive a new life, a new way of looking at the world. We *die* to an old life. We are "crucified with Christ," as Paul puts it. This is why the sign of the cross marked across our bodies on a regular basis is such a powerful devotional practice. We are freed from sin and death by going ahead and dying before we breathe our last.

8. *Regularly point out our national obsession with "winning."* I recently participated in the annual Multiple Sclerosis Walk in our city, walking with one of our members, Renate, who has suffered from MS for several decades now. She is a vocal supporter of the walk in our congregation. We often walk together and regularly finish near the end of the pack. Finishing last provides an interesting perspective. The walk was preceded by thirty minutes of rock music, dances including the Electric Slide, and inspirational speeches by speakers ranging from South Carolina Gamecock cheerleaders to the mayor. The herd of walkers was finally released in a rather frenzied state. Runners lapped us early on and were heard to remark, "We're winning! We're winning the MS walk!" It struck me that even in an event focusing on a disease that often leads to paralysis and death, a large number of the participants were caught up in finishing first. I've noticed a similar dynamic in hunger walks in our city. We'll do anything to distract us from the reality of disease and poverty that may very well lead to death, which is what we fear the most.

9. *Read large doses of good fiction.* Fiction writers often take holy time to enter into aspects of death that may be unfamiliar to pastors, especially those right out of seminary.

143

Listen to how Elizabeth Strout describes a young boy who has discovered his mother's suicide: "Kevin could not abide the thought of any child discovering what he had discovered; that his mother's need to devour her life had been so huge and urgent as to spray remnants of corporeality across the kitchen cupboards."[16] A single sentence describes a scene that still speaks volumes in the life of a boy now grown into a man who struggles with lingering depression.

Author Peter De Vries paints a wrenching scene in which a grief-stricken father whose young daughter would soon die brazenly throws a cake at a crucifix hanging over a church door.

> Outside, I paused on the sidewalk, one foot on the bottom step. I turned and looked up at the Figure still hanging as ever over the central doorway, its arms outspread among the sooted stones and strutting doves. I took the cake out of the box and balanced it a moment on the palm of my hand. Disturbed by something in the motion, the birds started from their covert and flapped away across the street. Then my arm drew back and let fly with all the strength within me.[17]

Finally, Annie Dillard describes a young man, John Ireland Sharp, whose entire family is drowned in a boating accident in Puget Sound in the 1870s, soon after his parents and siblings settle in that new and harsh landscape.

> They swayed like singers in a chorus under the pillars of the sea, enraptured in its vaults. Deep in his mind he followed them down and swayed to dirges with them there, for he had more taste for their company than he ever knew, and there was nothing to do up here on this dumb-show shore, in such a world, where people staked other people to the earth, and God pinned people under the sea among crabs.[18]

It is not necessary to quote from good fiction in the funeral homily to appreciate that writers like these have taken time to plumb the depths of human suffering and untimely death, bringing life's absurdities to honest speech. In many cases, such writers usher pastors like me into a foreign experience. Exposure to the many aspects of death and dying shapes the imagination of the preacher who is called to address agonies that will befall all our congregations if we stay in the business long enough. We'll see "car wrecks and measles and knives stuck in toasters, serial killers, burst appendices, bee stings, hard-candy chokings, croups untreated"—what Thomas Lynch calls "the aberrant disasters of childhood."[19] Good fiction writers wade unflinchingly into our shared mortality and prepare us for the inevitable death that arrives apart from natural sequence.

> When we bury the old, we bury the known past, the past we imagine sometimes better than it was, but the past all the same, a portion of which we inhabited. Memory is the overwhelming theme, the eventual comfort. But burying infants, we bury the future, unwieldly and unknown, full of promise and possibilities, outcomes punctuated by our rosy hopes. The grief has no borders, no limits, no known ends, and the little infant graves that edge the corners and fencerows of every cemetery are never quite big enough to contain that grief. Some sadnesses are permanent. Dead babies do not give us memories. They give us dreams.[20]

10. *Involve the congregation in the funeral sermon.* The funeral sermon, like any sermon, is an address to gathered worshipers who arrive in the pew with myriad questions, theologies, faiths (or the lack thereof), and memories. I recall one funeral of a beloved man in our congregation, Bob Stoudemire, who was known by many in the city as a former political science professor at the university, a rabid Democrat whose assortment of friends was truly representative of a good slice of the kingdom of God, and an unabashed cradle-

to-grave Lutheran who loved to spend his money supporting struggling future pastors who could not afford seminary tuition. Many people packed the sanctuary that day. Some were active churchgoers. Many were not. They all had in common a great love for Bob. He and his wife had no biological children during their long marriage, but then again it could be said that they had many children—a large family of friends made during a lifetime lived in a single region of the state.

I began the sermon that day by recounting an experience that many in the congregation could surely recall. I offer a bit of the sermon here not as a model homily but as an illustration of involving a very diverse congregation who shared a love for one man, who in turn loved an exceedingly greater man he named as Lord.

> If you ever had the opportunity to walk into Mary and Bob Stoudemire's yard on Lafayette Avenue in Cayce, you will recall stepping into a virtual rainbow of color—such a variety of flowers. Have you been there? Bob loved his books. They stretched from floor to ceiling in his den library. But I think he loved his bulbs and blossoms even more. A little bag of bulbs would always appear at my back door each planting season. There's a gospel message in that bag.
>
> I've been thinking about the first lesson today—God's rainbow in the clouds, God's promise to never again visit upon the earth a watery judgment. Bob chose this passage because he wanted us to remember his beloved "Army Rainbow Division" from World War Two. But perhaps he also had something else in mind. The rainbow in the sky is also a metaphor for this old professor's life—and a reflection of the diversity and variety of the kingdom of God he was a part of. Bob Stoudemire was many things: respected faculty member at USC, community leader, husband, friend. He was committed fiercely to the *polis*, the well-being of the city. But he was first and foremost a Christian.
>
> And when you truly follow Jesus and try to see all of life through the teachings and wide-angle lens of such a Lord,

then you're going to rattle a few cages and shake things up a bit during your days here on earth. Jesus says that his followers are supposed to be light and salt for this broken world. And Bob had the salty part down. After a speech in a faculty gathering or church council meeting, you never had to ask Bob if he would please be more forthcoming about his true feelings. He was a transparent disciple of Jesus, a straight shooter. He didn't believe in a Jesus who simply patted sheep in the pasture or held our hands with a soothing series of "there-there nows." Bob not only *believed* in Jesus; he dared to *follow* the man. There's a difference.

I remember several years ago at the height of the controversy in Cayce as Lutheran Family Services sought to resettle several Somali Bantu refugee families in the area. Bob was at breakfast one morning at a local establishment and overheard a table of his fellow citizens castigating the Lutherans for bringing such Bantu people into the community. Without batting an eye, Bob strode over to that table and said, "Let me tell you something. *I'm* a Lutheran. I'm a Lutheran and damn proud of it." And out the door he went, never turning around for a response, not needing their affirmation or howdy-do. No, Bob did not follow an edited, meek-and-mild version of Jesus. He had the fire of Jesus in him—the color, the pizzazz and passion of the gospel message under his skin. The gospel he lived included everybody, no matter their race, color, or creed. The variety in his flower garden spilled over into his life, his politics, his faith.

In the months before he moved to Lowman Home, Bob took me over to Compton's Kitchen in West Columbia for lunch several times. There's nothing fancy about the place— just great food, excellent pie. It was always filled to capacity at lunch, and they all knew Bob. He delighted in connecting with people, hearing their stories, knowing how they were doing. He loved being in the midst of such a variety of people from all walks of life sitting down to eat together.

I've thought many times about those lunches. Without saying so, I'm convinced that Dr. Stoudemire, our beloved Bob, was instructing me about life in the kingdom of God— about finding a place at God's table, the Lord's Table, where all are welcomed and gathered in. The only politics that really mattered for Bob had their grounding and basis in the Lord's Supper.

The food would arrive. He'd smile and wave at someone who'd just walked in. A flower at the center of the table, the center of his life. The One named Jesus now fully bloomed.

The Giving Tree

Every couple months or so I take a weekday afternoon and drive just south of the city to Congaree National Park for a prayer retreat. During Lent I block out an afternoon for prayer and preparation for the many services looming later in the season during Holy Week. I recall one Lenten Thursday I walked a couple miles in on the boardwalk, got off the boardwalk entirely and found a trail, then got off the trail and found a tree, completely out of sight. I sat under a massive bald cypress for a couple hours—praying, reading, noticing pileated woodpeckers (those prehistoric, red-headed birds), and the wild iris just beginning to poke through the soil. I was far from interstates and the noisy bustle of town. The bald cypress trees in Congaree are among the largest of their kind in eastern North America; if someone had come searching, it would have been hard to find me.

It's always good to be reminded of a natural order that keeps humming along without our notice or assistance— a seasonal rhythm set in place by a gracious and inventive hand. The huge tree that served as a backrest that Thursday was in existence long before I was born and will be around long after I breathe my last. In the summer, adult trees of this size sponge up *a ton of water* from the earth every day. One could almost hear this ancient granddaddy slurping a long, slow sip. I like to think of that astounding tree, see its branches silhouetted against the dim light of early evening. From a distance, its boughs appear as if they could hold a whole town—Swiss Family Columbia.

Down through the centuries of Christian history, the cross of Christ came to be known as a tree. Several times in the book of Acts, Luke doesn't use the common word *cross* but instead says something like, "They put him to death by hanging him on a tree" (10:39) or, "They took him down from the tree and laid him in a tomb" (13:29). So Clarence Jordan, in his "Cotton Patch Gospels," must have this image, in addition to a civil rights statement, in mind when he refers to Jesus's crucifixion as a lynching. I wonder if those who thought they could squelch our young nation's civil rights movement with violence knew that their chosen vehicle of death was actually connected to a very old and powerful metaphor—the cross as *tree*. "Happy are those who do not follow the advice of the wicked, or take the path that sinners tread, or sit in the seat of scoffers;[21] but their delight is in the law of the LORD, and on his law they meditate day and night. They are like trees planted by streams of water, which yield their fruit in its season, and their leaves do not wither. In all that they do, they prosper" (Ps. 1:1–3).

Saint Paul wrote, "Christ redeemed us from the curse of the law by *becoming* a curse for us—for it is written, 'Cursed is everyone who *hangs on a tree*'" (Gal. 3:13). Peter's correspondence puts it most graphically: "Christ carries up our sins in his body *to the tree*, so that we might live" (1 Pet. 2:24). Indeed, in early Christian tradition, the cross was understood to be planted *in the exact same place* where the Tree of Life once grew in the Garden of Eden. This tree will now have a new garden growing outward from its roots of grace. There is a great and mysterious paradox at work here. Jesus gives his life on a tree, but this tree in turn gives life to others.

149

If you've read Shel Silverstein's classic children's book *The Giving Tree*, you know that the author is tapping into powerful Christian themes that find their roots in the cross. The tree offers a boy branches for play, apples for snacks, shade for romance, wood for a house, a trunk for a boat, and finally a stump to sit on. The tree was always happy to give whatever it had, without complaint. The tree in the story is a sacrificial symbol suggesting that we are offered life as a sheer, unconditional gift. The cross of Christ is our "Giving Tree." Jesus holds nothing back.

At the height of El Salvador's long civil war, a story of a massacre in the small village of El Mozote, not far from where one of my daughters was born, surfaced. I quote here from the account:

> There was one in particular the soldiers talked about that evening, a girl whom they had raped many times during the course of the afternoon, and through it all, while the other women of El Mozote had screamed and cried . . . this girl had sung hymns, strange evangelical songs, and she had kept right on singing, even after they had done what had to be done, and shot her in the chest. She had lain there on La Cruz with the blood flowing from her chest, and had kept on singing—a bit weaker than before, but still singing. And the soldiers, stupefied, had watched and pointed. Then they had grown tired of the game and shot her again, and she sang still, and their wonder began to turn to fear—until finally they unsheathed their machetes and hacked through her neck, and at last the singing stopped.[22]

There are images in the Gospels in which Jesus cries out to God in pain and doubt. There are images in which he sweats drops of blood agonizingly in the garden. But you will not find them in John's account. There the powerful begin to wonder about another power this man has even in dying, their wonder, like that of the soldiers standing over that little girl, "turning to fear."

If the tree is still living, is there any earthly power more powerful than the presence of Christ in our lives? Are we not grafted through baptism into the same family tree as our Lord? As one pastor puts it, "A faith that is well-grounded has an evenness about it. It doesn't rise and fall with the Dow Jones average or the inflection of a physician's voice. Why, in the eyes of faith, would you entertain adding a dimension of panic to your prayers tomorrow when it's not in them today? Shouldn't the gratitude and hope that are part of your spiritual life today be perfectly suited for tomorrow?"[23]

Every Lent on Whitetop Mountain in Virginia (near where I used to live), residents bore into the maple trees and out flows the sweet sap. In John's passion narrative, as Jesus hangs on the tree, breathing his last, soldiers pierce his side with a spear. Out comes blood. And water. Humanity pierces the side of Jesus, bores into the tree of life, and out flows the sweet love of chalice and font. Even in death, Jesus nourishes the world.

This tree metaphor informs a powerful vision of the Bible's final chapter. You've heard it: "Then the angel showed me the river of the water of life, bright as crystal, flowing from the throne of God and of the lamb through the middle of the street of the city. On either side of the river is *the tree of life* . . . and the leaves of the tree are for the healing of the nations" (Rev. 22:1–2).

The leaves of the tree. Who are they? The leaves of the tree are surely God's people, rooted in the love of the cross, growing for the sake of the world. We are born in Christ for such healing.

There is an ancient tree on a hill just outside Jerusalem— much older and bigger than the bald cypress tree I leaned against in Congaree National Park. On it hangs a man, in silence, with arms outstretched. Rings of love inside the tree reveal the height and width and depth of the tree's reach toward the earth's four directions—concentric circles of grace, moving ever outward. The tree, once planted in sin, now grows in love. And a new garden blossoms forth.

Around dusk I like to look back over the day, back over my life, and see the long braches of this tree silhouetted against the evening's last light. From a distance, the tree looks like it could hold the whole world in its sturdy boughs.

Here's the gospel truth: it can.

7

Remaining in Ephesus

Speaking the Truth with Councils and Vestries

I urge you as I did when I was on the way to Macedonia, to remain in Ephesus so that you may instruct certain people not to teach any different doctrine, and not to occupy themselves with myths and endless genealogies that promote speculations rather than divine training that is known by faith.

1 Timothy 1:3–4

And now, Lord, look at their threats, and grant to your servant to speak your word with all boldness, while you stretch out your hand to heal, and signs and wonders are performed through the name of your holy servant Jesus.

Acts 4:29–30

Barbara Brown Taylor tells a story of a retreat she once attended. The leader asked the group to think of an instance when someone reached out in a way that reminded them of the actions of Jesus in the Gospels. Several people stood and recalled various acts of kindness: a compassionate visit in the hospital, a stranger stopping to provide roadside assistance, a particular teacher who taught the class about love and charity. There was a very quiet woman in the group who had not said much the entire weekend. She stood and said, "I had to think hard about that one. I kept thinking, 'Who is it who told me the truth about myself so clearly that I wanted to kill him for it?'"[1]

Lutheran pastors are called each month to tell the truth about congregational life to various leaders who make up a board, council, or vestry. Most of us are given time in our monthly report to share news about parish life, specific prayer concerns, and upcoming events. But the report is also a time to share honestly about where we are as a church and where we are going. Reporting sometimes results in hurt feelings and stepped-on toes.

I serve at Ebenezer Church, a large downtown parish blessed with a beautiful neo-Gothic worship space. Organized in 1830, the church became known as the mother church of the South Carolina Synod in our denomination. Like many urban congregations, we are a church in transition and no longer the force we once were in the community. There are many reasons for this, notably population shifts, the challenge of being the church in the city, and membership rolls that span many zip codes. Very few of our members live near the church building. We are a "destination church" in many ways and struggle to build meaningful community because our members are so far-flung.

Not the Messiah: Learning from John the Baptist

When I was a teenager, it always seemed like my dad would pepper me with a thousand questions whenever we were alone

154

together. His conversational probing would invariably drive me crazy because teenagers often need lots of quiet, brooding time to ruminate upon life and romance and the future. As teens we were pretty certain that any adult within a fifty-mile radius hadn't a clue about any of the things that mattered to us.

As it often happens, I've turned into my father in this regard. "Did you have fun? Well, who was there? Anybody I know? So where does she hope to go to school next fall? Do you like his parents? What do they do? What are they like?" And it's just the subtle eye roll that lets me know I've gone too far too fast in the interrogation. For that is what this has become. And thirty-five years vanish, and I'm the teenager again, remembering the feeling of being trapped and cross-examined by a parent in the front seat of a moving automobile.

I suppose John the Baptist had plenty of room to run that day, to escape, as his interrogators assembled (John 1:19–28). It was a long river and a big wilderness, so I suppose John could have just outrun them all and hidden out in a cave for a few days. But he chose to stay.

I recall the first months of my new call to Columbia. I lived in an apartment from February to June, until my family could join me that summer. I would wake every morning at 4:00 a.m. and stare at the ceiling, convinced I'd made a huge mistake. I had a strong urge to run back to the familiarity of my old parish in Virginia. I could pack up the apartment, count my books over at the church office as a loss, and be back home by mid-morning. The urge to pack up and rejoin my family tugged on my pastoral soul for many weeks. But I stayed.

John stays too, and the cadre of questioners assembles on the banks of the Jordan, careful not to get their shoes wet, and the questions start flying one after another. If John feels trapped by these people, like a teenager trapped in a car by a well-meaning parent, he doesn't show it. "Who are you? Are you Elijah? Are you the prophet? What do you say about yourself? We need some explanation for those who sent us. Why are you baptizing if you're not the Messiah, nor Elijah, nor the Prophet?" You can almost feel the riverbank assemblage lean in for the answers, ready to nail him.

John's responses to the pointed questions are deceptively brief and elusive. "I am not," he replies to one question. "Nope," to another. In answer to one question he even says, "I am the voice." I am the voice? His answer might've seemed as helpful as "I am the Artist Formerly Known as Prince." John is brief. He says what he means. He refuses to elaborate about himself. He prefers to point to someone else.

I don't know if you've had to complete a resume for a congregation call committee lately. Most of the time it's an exercise in putting your best foot forward. But who would hire John the Baptist? Who would approve him for ordination? He refuses to talk about himself. He consistently insists upon defining himself in terms of somebody else. "Who are you?" asks the nice lady behind the interview desk. "I am a witness to the light," he answers. "I am the voice of one crying out in the wilderness." She pushes the silent alarm button.

In answer to one question about his identity, John says who he is not. "I am not the Messiah." I've found John's answer to be a particularly poignant posture for living a healthy life. Not that anyone would confuse a pastor for the Messiah, of course, but it's still tempting sometimes for a pastor to try to be one. Maybe you've tried to save a family member from addiction or from some behavior that's killing them. Perhaps you've tried to save a marriage that's spiraling out of control and headed toward divorce. Maybe you've been particularly passionate about a project that's important to you, but no one else seems to care.

In a variety of situations, I've found it very important to say, "I am not the Messiah." As a member of the clergy, it's easy to feel that the success of the congregation falls on my shoulders. It doesn't. Which is not to say that the Messiah does not need you and me. But it's critical to make sure we've got this straight in a variety of situations (and more than you might think): "I am not the Messiah." This is a particularly good thing to remember as we begin a relationship with a new congregation and church council leaders with whom we provide mission oversight and implementation. A lot of expectations hover around a new pastor.

John the Baptist stands beside an old river and finds himself peppered with questions. Maybe you can envision yourself standing there with him. For these are our questions too. The church's mission depends on faithful answers.

Desired Outcomes

Since 2006, we at Ebenezer Lutheran have been working with the Alban Institute and one of their very helpful consultants, Ed White. Ed has helped us devise a list of desired outcomes that serve as a blueprint for our long-range planning and mission:

A. Ebenezer will live its mission so that it will be a beacon (a light on a hill) that is known in the community for exhibiting the love of Christ. Guests will be sought out and specifically welcomed by members. Strangers and newcomers, including the homeless, will experience consistent hospitality in our church.

B. The congregation will develop a local, on-the-street reputation as a Spirit-tuned congregation where a diversity of people—unbaptized adults, people who question, skeptics, and religious seekers—might come to explore Christianity. The reputation will develop as member/disciples grow in their ability to welcome and share their faith beyond the doors of the church building.

C. The church will be a gathering place with opportunities for youth and young adults to meet, grow, and explore their faith and faithfulness. Development of this outcome will occur through staff configuration and the support of member/disciples as they grow in understanding the unique opportunities of a downtown congregation to attract younger member/disciples.

D. In worship, the people gathered will experience the living God and not merely hear about him. They will be strengthened through a personal relationship between God and humanity and grow in faithfulness.

E. Lutheran liturgy will be interpreted in worship to explain and emphasize its meaning and place in our beliefs, practices, and traditions.

F. Variety in worship will honor the cultures, languages, and generations of the participating worshipers.

G. The word *Jesus* will be on the lips of Ebenezer member/disciples more than the word *Ebenezer*. Ultimately, this will translate into a congregation of disciples who are outward looking and acting—people sent out to share Christ at work, home, and at play, people who bring Good News by serving the poor, the imprisoned, and the oppressed in tangible ways (Luke 4:18–19).

H. We will be a gifts-based community where spiritual gifts are discerned, celebrated, and named as an act of discipleship that expresses one's love for God. Members will feel a sense of call to give consistently of their time, talents, and resources.

I. We will develop meaningful relationships with one another through a community of small groups of seven to eight people (meeting weekly over a specific period of time) linked by a combination of prayer, Bible study, mutual support, and specific mission to the congregation and community.

J. Christian education is a life cycle process, and Ebenezer will offer year-round opportunities, not merely those paralleling the school year. Study curriculum will be biblically based and Lutheran-centered, with subjects appealing to the whole spectrum of those participating.

K. Adult members will be well-grounded in the Scriptures and discipleship so that through faith and by example they can nurture the children and youth in Christian formation. In this way the generations will understand and value one another.

L. The physical campus will be maintained and enhanced for the sake of faithful ministry, welcome, and hospitality.

Our church council has courageously and consistently taken the lead in seeing the need for an outside consultant, and we have made good headway in addressing a variety of the outcomes. But we've had our bumps in the road along the way.

Where Is the Power?

Four Old Testament passages serve as key texts as Ebenezer's pastors and council members work to implement the desired outcomes we've sketched for our future together.

Exodus 18:13–23. Jethro, Moses's father-in-law, asks him one of the key questions of biblical leadership in this story. "Why do you sit alone, while all the people stand around you from morning until evening?" (v. 14). Jethro surely speaks the truth to his son-in-law, who is running around trying to please everyone. "You will surely wear yourself out, both you and these people with you. For the task is too heavy for you; you cannot do it alone" (v. 18). It's interesting that Jethro warns against burnout not only for the haggard leader but also for those the leader is trying to serve! Going it alone helps no one in the long run. Jethro's instructions to Moses to equip others to "bear the burden with you" (v. 18:22) are wisely heeded by leaders in any century.

Part of the regular task of speaking the truth in love with church council leaders is holding each other accountable to the simple truth that we're in this together. It is very easy to slide into destructive habits in which a pastor sits in on every meeting and consults on every decision. Micromanagement is a particular hazard for pastors, not so much because we want control but because often it's easier in the short run to take care of the myriad details in parish ministry ourselves. In the long run, however, being involved in every aspect of church management will spell disaster for one's emotional health and subvert the important calls of the laity who are on church council to lead and not just to rubber-stamp the plans of a pastor. Regular, honest self-examination can be helpful. How am I spending my time? Am I doing things that could (and should) be accomplished by someone else? Learning to delegate has taken a long time for me, since I came from a smaller rural parish to serve in a much larger congregation. A faithful church council can function like Jethro for any pastor, asking honestly and regularly if what we are doing as pastors truthfully serves the long-range goals we've agreed upon.

1 Kings 19:4–9. For any leader (pastor or council) there will be peaks and valleys as he or she works through long-range plans. It is startling how quickly even the prophet Elijah moves from incredible success with the prophets of Baal in 1 Kings 18 to dark depression following the threats of an upstaged Jezebel in 1 Kings 19.

At Ebenezer Church we have just gone through our own version of the worship wars—where the very worst in behaviors emerged following a change in our Sunday morning schedule. Numerous phone calls were made. Questions about pastoral allegiance to the call contract were asked. Concerns about the process we used in arriving at an interim schedule as a staffing search for a new music minister was under way were voiced. Preferences about musical style overriding parish unity were made known. And on and on. It was an incredibly exhausting time and required untold amounts of pastoral energy and worry. If you really want to test a congregation's spirit of unity, fiddle around with the Sunday morning worship schedule for several months. Our council eventually voted to return to the previous schedule, not out of faithfulness to our desired outcomes but in an attempt to please as many people as possible, fearful that many would leave if we didn't return to the way things were. I honestly thought of leaving during this period. I wanted to retreat (Elijah-like) into my own little cave and call it quits. I daydreamed about searching the want ads for new employment.

Part of speaking the truth in love means that church leaders (pastors and councils) will not always get their way. How do we live together when inevitable conflict arises? In the Elijah story, it is the angelic visitor arriving with physical contact and heavenly bread for the journey that eventually shakes our hero out of his leadership funk. We will disagree with and disappoint one another in any congregational ministry that matters. It is the Eucharist and the heavenly bread of Christ that ultimately unite us and allow us to move forward even as we disagree.

Nehemiah 8:1–3, 8–12. After the Babylonian exile, with Jerusalem in ruins, Ezra and Nehemiah seek to rebuild. A key

161

narrative within the larger story of rebuilding occurs when the people assemble at the Water Gate (v. 1). They listen to the priest, Ezra, read from Scripture "from early in the morning until midday, in the presence of the men and the women and those who could understand" (v. 3). They are completely immersed in the Word of God. Immersion is central to any project of renewal in any congregation and pivotal for shaking leadership out of the Elijah-like doldrums that can happen to any of us. If any council member in a position of leadership is not immersed in the Word of God through regular and even daily study, it is fair to ask why not. Questioning new council members about their Scripture intake in an interview format could be a fair part of the nominating process each fall. Much of the friction that emerges in council meetings stems from the fact that people aren't on the same page biblically speaking. Writes Walter Brueggemann:

> The world of the Bible consists in a dispute about evidence. The baptized community is "in the dock," summoned to tell the truth and not to bear false witness. The preacher, moreover, is regularly and visibly put on exhibit, to tell the church's truth to the world and to tell God's truth to the church. Very often the world refuses to hear, and of course the church is regularly recalcitrant in receiving testimony. And even the preacher, on occasion, cringes from what must be said, so much are we ourselves accommodated to "the lie."[2]

Esther 4:4–17. Esther soon learns that she has not been chosen as queen for her looks alone. Her courageous intervention on behalf of her people will involve great risk, but "who knows? Perhaps you have come to royal dignity for just such a time as this" (v. 14). After recognizing a shared call, the reality of ministerial ups and downs, and the necessity of complete immersion in Scripture, councils are then called to take a risk and move forward, even if this means the death of long-held patterns of ministry in a particular congregation.

These Scripture stories become templates of leadership for councils to which all concerned are held accountable. One question needs constant revisiting among leaders: where is the power? Is the power in members whose families have held sway for generations? Is the power in certain wealthy members who annually rescue the budget and need to be kept happy? Is the power in the pastoral office? Does this result in always giving the pastor what he or she wants? Is the power (as in our case) a mile up the road at the State House? Council leaders must learn to reckon with this question, ask it often, and come to realize that the power is in a story older than any of us, found in the pages of Scripture, and revealed in the crucified and risen Christ. Christ is our power. If council leaders are not immersed in the story, they will not recognize the import of the question posed to Esther, nor will they have the biblical gumption to take risks and make potentially unpopular decisions. There is another way to pose this question about the locus of power: whom are we attempting to please? An honest answer to this question almost always reveals the source of a congregation's true power, for better or for worse.

Daniel and Pastoral Leadership in a Foreign Land

If Jethro, Elijah, Nehemiah, and Esther serve as biblical role models for council leadership struggling with issues of true power, the book of Daniel is a key text for pastoral leadership, particularly the sixth chapter.

"Because an excellent spirit was in him" (Dan. 6:3), Daniel the foreigner emerges in Babylon as a leader among leaders in the court of King Darius. When considering pastoral leadership in a local congregation, it's important not to neglect the fact that we are, in many respects, foreigners called to serve a culture that has been humming along (for over 175 years in my case) with a set of habits that may or may not have anything to do with authentic biblical witness. It will take some time for insiders to trust a foreigner who comes with new ideas, no matter how truthfully or artfully the ideas are packaged. And even then there will always be a group that does not like the changes and in truth does not like the foreigner. "Woe to you when all speak well of you," says Jesus (Luke 6:26). Grumbling against the pastor may well signal progress in drawing close to the way of Jesus. Those used to a certain system will try mightily "to find grounds for complaint" (Dan. 6:4) against the new and foreign leader.

In just under seven years of service in my present call, I have been accused of taking too much time away from the parish. My call contract has been requested and examined to make sure I'm doing all agreed-upon acts of ministry. Hours have been spent on the phone in response to a baptismal request I denied. Issues like these can slowly erode a pastor's excitement for ministry and sense of call. Many pastors are leaving their posts fewer than five years in because the "grounds for complaint" seem to swirl incessantly. Seminaries should better prepare ministers for the fact that there will always be a group who "conspire" (Dan. 6:6, literally, "to breathe together") against new ideas and new leadership. If an idea is truly of God and if Satan is alive and well in the world today, conflict will raise its ugly head. Pastors who are doing a good job should expect conflict. There is really no way for Jesus to come into lives without large doses of change, and change will bring division. Will Willimon echoes this idea: "The real reason people get upset with preachers is not your management style, but that you represent Jesus. The purpose of preaching is to provide proper division on the basis of the gospel."[3] So expect conspiratorial faction groups in the church. Their existence means you are doing your job.

We see evidence of evil at work in Daniel's story too. Those who conspire against Daniel set a trap for him. "Whoever prays to anyone, divine or human, for thirty days, except to you, O King, shall be thrown into a den of lions" (Dan. 6:7). And, in truth, Daniel was already in their den. Here again is an opportunity for the pastoral leader to ask the vital question: *Where is the power?* Daniel, fully aware of the trap, becomes as transparent as humanly possibly in his answer. "He continued to go to his house, which had *windows* in its upper rooms" (6:10), and prayed three times a day, just as he always had. Daniel doesn't seem to give a fig about the power play of the conspirators. He relies on the old habits, the tradition of his spiritual forebears.

Daniel is eventually tossed among the real lions and emerges unscathed. He knows the true power. And his faithful and courageous witness changes the culture of that community. Whole families are demoted (6:24). Those who thought they had the power (even the king of the community) discover a higher power: "For he is the living God, enduring forever. His kingdom shall never be destroyed, and his dominion has no end. He delivers and rescues, he works signs and wonders in heaven and on earth; for he has saved Daniel from the power of the lions" (6:26–27).

Chapter 6 in Daniel is all about appropriate divisions in communities of faith. History and established power will often combine to create a perfect storm seeking to thwart new directions of the spirit. Recall that in Acts the believers and apostles "criticized" Peter (11:2) for eating with folk outside the prescribed norms of the faith. Councils and vestries are often timid about bucking tradition and "the way we have always done things here." That some division is okay flies in the face of the familiar perception church councils sometimes have of themselves as keepers of the peace who please as many people as possible and are prone to focus on two numbers measuring success: the budget and average church attendance. Part of our calling as the "foreigner" is to preach Jesus so faithfully, truthfully, and courageously that some people (notably the conspirators) may leave. "Pastors are called to *testify*, not become false peacemakers. This will bring conflict when people realize Caesar isn't Lord."[4]

Remaining in Ephesus or Crete

In the midst of congregational conflict surrounding a shift in allegiance to the true power that is Christ, siren voices will emerge and attempt to convince pastors that the situation is hopeless and the best tack is to leave and seek another congregation. There may come a time when it is appropriate to leave a parish in the midst of conflict, but I'm more and more convinced that such an inclination comes from a voice other than God's. Satan's subtle voice works constantly to perpetuate false power. Time and again in his letters to young pastors, Paul urges his charges to stay put. "Remain in Ephesus," he says to Timothy, even though the young pastor is obviously frustrated with his current post (1 Tim. 1:3). Titus is fed up with the Cretans and ready to leave the island once and for all when he receives a letter from Paul, who says there is much work remaining to be done. The pastor's work includes silencing "rebellious people" (Titus 1:10), teaching "sound doctrine" (2:2), urging "self-control" to the young (2:6) and "reverence in behavior" (2:3) to the old. Why? "Because the grace of God has appeared, bringing salvation to all, training us to renounce impiety and worldly passions, and in the present age to live lives that are self-controlled, upright and godly" (2:11–12).

In a sermon published in 1933, "Making the Best of a Bad Mess," Harry Emerson Fosdick names our desire to flee:

> Let us put ourselves in Titus' place. It ought not to be difficult. One way or another we are always getting into Crete. There are so many differences that separate us here this morning, but any preacher could be sure of one thing which unites us: we have all been in Crete, we are all going to be in Crete, probably most of us are in Crete now. Moreover, we are human and complaining, and we want to get out of Crete.[5]

It is tempting for pastors to vilify and become disappointed with an entire congregation (or group of leaders). "Cretans are always liars, vicious brutes, lazy gluttons" (Titus 1:12). Always? In truth, we are usually dealing with a handful of troublemakers who pretend to speak for a much larger group that is nonexistent. Paul writes, "I left you behind in Crete for this reason, so that you should put in order what remained to be done" (1:5). "What remains to be done" cannot be accomplished quickly. Do not flee quickly from important conflict. Chances are, you're making some headway there on Crete or in Ephesus or wherever the Spirit has led you for "just such a time as this" (Esther 4:14).

Conclusion

Why Church Members Need More than a Chaplain Who Cares

Whoever says, "I have come to know him," but does not obey his commandments, is a liar, and in such a person the truth does not exist.

1 John 1:4

Truth-seeking is also arduous. The most insidious form of sloth for me personally is busyness. Busyness impedes the business of truth. Staying too busy at daily professional tasks means not stilling the mind enough to know what we really think, not thinking things through, not following speculation to its sometimes unwelcome conclusion, not picking at that unsatisfactory sentence until the whole piece comes unraveled.[1]

Margaret A. Miller

If busyness does indeed impede truth, then a pastor may be the chief of impeders. It is easy to justify our presence in the parish via schedule and appointment. It's easy to race through a day of hospital visits, counseling appointments,

169

Bible studies, worship preparation, and crisis calls. It is easy to go about dispensing nuggets of spiritual wisdom, holding a hand, offering a well-timed prayer but never daring to speak the truthful (and sometimes difficult) Word of God. Eugene Peterson has humorously noted that, given six months, he could produce a pastor that most congregations would dearly love. The abbreviated seminary curriculum would consist of just four courses: (1) Creative Plagiarism; (2) Voice Control for Prayer and Counseling; (3) Efficient Office Management; and (4) Image Projection: "A one-week refresher course each year would introduce new phrases that would convince our parishioners that we are bold innovators on the cutting edge of the megatrends and at the same time solidly rooted in all the traditional values of our sainted ancestors."[2]

Each of the previous five chapters addressed a common area of weekly clergy life. Taken together, these areas produce a busy life all by themselves. When you add to the mix political fallout, the need for explanation, and criticism by laypeople and church leaders, it's easy to see why pastors come to resemble the quivering mass of availability described in the doctor's waiting room at the onset of this book. They are reduced to vessels into which woes are poured. But what if our task is to assist people with the startling claim in 1 John 1:3? "We will be like him." *We will be like Jesus.* Given that this is the Holy Spirit's project in us all, how do pastors assist the Spirit? How is hand-holding and caring simply not sufficient for leading parishioners into the truth of Christ? I want to close this book on pastoral truth telling by examining closely two scriptural paradigms—one describing birth and the other describing growth.

War of Words

When I was a little boy, my Aunt Flossie once took me fishing in nearby Chickamauga Creek in Chattanooga. My parents were away somewhere, and she was watching me that weekend until they returned. We sat on a bridge above the creek and dropped a cork into the water with a hook hidden by a fat ball of Wonder Bread. I was after carp, and sure enough a lazy, fat one swam to the top. I kept barely missing the fish as it sucked the bread off my hook with those fat carp lips that were used to digesting all sorts of stuff off the creek bottom, including nails. It was agonizing for a little boy to see that wondrous fish so close and slow and yet to keep missing, missing, missing. Once I jerked the line so hard that the hook and bobber flew out of the water and got caught in the tree limbs far above our heads.

But just as we were about to leave, I hooked that carp. The fish dove deep toward the creek bottom, and my rod bent double. I pulled him up hand over hand until the great fish was flopping on the bridge. And I was so excited. Most people don't keep carp, but I wanted to show this fish to my uncle when he got home from work. I was afraid he wouldn't believe me, I guess. I begged until Aunt Flossie relented. She had a half-gallon orange juice container in her car. One of the abiding images from that day is riding home in the backseat of my aunt's car with a large fish tail flopping out of a container that would no longer be used to pour orange juice. My uncle seemed excited about the catch when he got home from work, but I noticed he grumbled later that evening when he headed out to the woods with the now-silent fish and a shovel.

● ● ●

Pastors know a great deal about the power of words—their power to create or destroy (Jer. 1:9–10), their power to tap into the imagination, their power to evoke entire worlds and old memories from the subconscious. Perhaps as you read my childhood story of hooking a carp, you recalled for an instant a field trip of your own, or remembered the kindness of a favorite aunt, or conjured a time from long ago when you were so excited to show someone something that you could've burst. Evocative words have the power to create whole new worlds. One of the reasons we read good fiction is not so much to escape or find fleeting entertainment in a busy world but to figure out how the world works, indeed how *we* work.

A serious reader of words, an intent and patient listener to words, will be formed by them—you might even say be created by them. There have been certain books in my life without which I would not be the same person. Words properly ingested have the potential of shaping us into people we could never become *without* the words. Indeed, God *speaks* the world into being in the first chapter of Genesis. Let there be light. Let there be wildebeest. "Christians," writes Tom Long, "don't just say things because they believe them to be true. God's truth is more complex than mere factuality. Words do things, words cause things to happen, words have consequences, and Christians take those consequences into account when speaking the truth."[3]

The challenge in speaking God's truth is that we live in a culture absolutely flooded with words. One of the reasons I have largely stopped watching television over the last twenty years is that TV, in so many cases, cheapens words. We live in a world so awash in words, many of them insipid and de-meaning, that we're able to accomplish several things at once (multitasking[4] as it's called) while words fly all around us, almost without our notice. The lack of silence in our lives has created an entire culture that is rapidly losing the ability to listen to words with any real and meaningful discernment.

In 1858, for the first Lincoln-Douglas debate, the format was the following: Douglas spoke for an hour, Lincoln followed with a ninety-minute reply, then Douglas followed with a half-hour rebuttal. If that's not enough to make our modern rear ends numb, previous debates between the two were over twice as long and included a break for dinner. Their audiences were not exceptionally well-educated listeners, just common people who took politics and the common good seriously. Neil Postman asks, "Is there any audience of Americans today who could endure seven hours of talk? Or five? Or three? Especially without pictures of any kind?"[5]

Even in the din of commercialized, contemporary life, certain words can still command immediate attention and create whole and instantaneous new worlds. Take these two words you've perhaps shared with your children: "We're moving." Take these few words I heard several New Year's Days ago about a good friend: "George has been shot." Take the words not a few of us have heard about those we love: "The tumor is malignant."

"In the beginning was the Word, and the Word was with God, and the Word was God" (John 1:1). I have a strong suspicion that anyone who refers to the creator of the universe as "the Word" has a pretty elevated understanding of the power of human and divine speech and the importance of words in general to bring about new birth in our lives. "And the Word *was* God." Everything was created, claims John, through this Word. And indeed it's this very Word that "became" flesh. John chooses to begin his Gospel in exactly the same way as the author of Genesis: "In the beginning . . ." Something new is being created, and it has to do with words. Martin Luther once said that the Word of God is the manger where Christ is born in our hearts.

There is war raging all around clergy leaders these days—the war of words. Certain words are competing for our attention, pulling us slowly away from the Word of Life. Pastors

173

become content with canned words, soothing words, and words that never rock the boat.

Oil Shortage and Christian Growth

Of all the religious jokes that have been told wherever Christians gather, perhaps the most popular are "Saint Peter at the Pearly Gate" jokes. A whole joke genre has developed around a man who stands guard at the gates of heaven and checks entrance credentials. Saint Peter has become the comedic, divine Santa Claus—the bearded man in white who at the end of time checks his list and then checks it twice. He can see right there who's been naughty or nice. Lutherans in particular love Saint Peter jokes, I think, because we know in truth that salvation doesn't work this way. It's a gift rather than something to be earned. So we laugh and indulge rather lustily at the punch lines, knowing that entrance into heaven is through grace alone.

Trouble is, nobody's laughing in the old lesson of the ten bridesmaids (Matt. 25:1–13). The punch line doesn't seem so funny—five are whooping it up at a marriage feast, but five others are shut out, left completely in the cold. The words of the bridegroom are as ominous as any in the entire Bible: "I do not know you." And the door swings shut like some huge castle door that creaks on its hinges until—*bam!* On one side of the door is a party. On the other side, darkness. Half make it, half don't. Isn't that the trouble with the Bible sometimes? We think we've got God all figured out, think we're all cozy and chummy, swapping jokes and laughing, and then something like this startles our sensibilities.

Does this story bother you? I must admit that it bothers me a great deal. It's hard for me to envision a loving Jesus leaving anybody out, especially people who are knocking at the door, *pleading* to get in. "Lord, please open to us." And he won't. Why won't those stingy girls share any of their oil? Is that any sort of model Christian behavior? And the bridegroom doesn't say boo about their apparent stinginess. What's so confounded important about the oil anyway?

As evidenced in the parable of the bridesmaids, there is judgment in the Bible. It's not all bouncing sheep and promises of paradise. The prophet Amos speaks for God and angrily exposes those who rely on worship and ritual and yet ignore matters of injustice and poverty and peace. God is nauseated by the faithful who go through weekly religious motions and tip their little Sabbath caps to God but exhibit precious little evidence that their daily lives have much to do with God at all. An hour of sis-boom-bah apparently doesn't do much to appease the Big Guy in the sky. It apparently doesn't do much to please the living God. God's words can be so hot and fiery that a blast of his anger can singe your eyebrows. "I hate, I despise your festivals," says God, never one to mince words. "Take away from me the noise of your little songs, your blathering hymns, your insipid sermons. Your worship life," says God in so many words, "has precious little to do with your daily life. It's justice I'm after: care of the poor, radical sharing with those who have nothing. Let justice roll down like waters, and righteousness like an ever-flowing stream. If your worship doesn't lead to justice, take it away from me. I can do without it" (see Amos 5:21–24).

We know there is judgment in the Bible. But sometimes we think it's only reserved for *somebody else*, for obviously bad and sinful people, terrorists like Osama bin Laden, tyrants like the now-deposed Saddam Hussein. It's very easy for me to be lulled by the news and say, "I may have my little faith indiscretions, but at least I'm not as messed up as that guy." We sometimes receive a kind of sick reassurance from

175

examining where we fall in the moral order of things. There's even a demonic inner glee (you've felt it) when someone you don't particularly like happens to mess up. Our hearts leap a little at another's demise.

So maybe you like this old parable, at least a little. It's a judgment parable. It might just reinforce a common notion that some (like us) will make it and others (fill in the blank here) won't. The parable gives us a place to put them: on the other side of the door, in the dark where they belong.

Generally speaking, in any society, any culture, if we can eliminate the obvious infidel, the heinous sinner, the trouble-making outsider, then, according to conventional wisdom, our problems will go away. Doesn't matter if we're talking about homeless people, homosexuals, or Muslims. If we can attach some sort of accepted accusation to a target group, then it's easier to vilify that group. So we hear things like, "All homeless people are lawless and messy and trashy," or "All homosexuals are child abusers," or "All Muslim people have terrorist leanings." All these statements are silly, impossibly wrongheaded. But they are also extremely common. Right up to the eve of the national election, there was a massive effort across the nation to discredit President Obama with the charge that he is a Muslim and not to be trusted. I almost cheered when General Colin Powell finally came out and said, "What if he was? What if he's not a Christian? Does that somehow discredit his candidacy in this nation?"

This judgment parable from Matthew loudly refutes claims suggesting some outside, sinister presence as the source of all our problems. In fact, God doesn't take aim at outsiders at all in this story. God's anger is levied instead at *insiders*. God's judgment is upon people like us—good churchgoing people who have allowed a host of other concerns to crowd God to the margins of life. This is a huge theme in both testaments.

It's not the obvious sinner, the outside threat, who regularly commands God's attention. *It's the apathy and infidelity of those who follow the dominant faith.*

All ten bridesmaids in this story are insiders. Please notice that. They all have lamps. They all are on their way to meet the bridegroom. They all are dressed the same way and heading to the same party. They all fall asleep together when the bridegroom, who is undoubtedly Jesus, is delayed. They all are insiders. It's an ominous story, a story of judgment. "And the door was shut." *Clang.* But I have to wonder. Who is really rejecting whom in this old tale? Jesus is not slamming the door in anyone's face. Jesus is simply telling the truth. "I don't know you." Apparently there will come a time when Jesus tells us whether our relationship with him does or does not truly exist.

The foolish bridesmaids, after they've run out of oil, want to borrow some from the wise. The answer they receive seems selfish, but, in truth, somebody else cannot hand a relationship with Christ to another person. No one can believe, tithe, worship, pray, study, or serve for someone else. Parents often learn this truth painfully as their children get older. There comes a point when a child makes his or her own decision to accept or reject the faith. "Give us some of your oil, for our lamps are going out." Sadly, faith cannot be loaned or borrowed. Each of us must do business with God and engage in practices that foster a deep relationship. No one can do that for you.

Sometimes well-meaning Christians have a nasty habit of letting others know how horrible outsiders—Hindus, illegal immigrants, prisoners, and the assortment of bad people in the news—are. But the parable of the bridesmaids is not addressed to somebody else. It's not told so an atheist might wise up and come to Jesus. The parable is for insiders like us. It's a wake-up call for good church people. "I don't know you," says the bridegroom. His statement is not a threat. The parable doesn't say the five foolish ones are going to hell. But there will come a day, apparently, when Jesus declares whether or not our relationship with him truly exists, whether or not the relationship has borne fruit, whether or not he truly knows us. Please notice. He doesn't say, "I do not love you." He doesn't say, "I never tried to get your attention." He says, "I don't *know* you." He is stating the truth of the matter. Christians who think they can party with Jesus without taking seriously his challenging teachings in their lives are fooling themselves. For Christians, rebirth without growth is a half-truth. Pastors are called to interrupt the dangerous lie of proclaiming justification apart from sanctification.

To Tell the Truth

I had breakfast recently with a pastoral colleague who lamented, "The hardest thing about ministry in my setting is that we've got so many members who are spiritually ill-equipped to deal with a crisis in their lives. People get sick or face a death in the family or the marriage falls apart, and they come to me and want to know where God is in all that. Which is fine, of course. They expect me to be there and I should be. But what strikes me so often is that they seem to have very few spiritual resources with which to deal with the crisis, very little biblical depth to draw upon. I sometimes feel as if I'm little more than a hired chaplain, on call for folk who think about God only in an emergency. By then there's little I can do except hold hands and listen."

Contrast the word *chaplain* with the word *pastor*. A chaplain typically provides a religious presence for an institution such as a hospital, a prison, the Navy, Congress, or the Elk's

Club. Don't get me wrong. I have nothing against chaplains. They provide hints of God in sterile settings for those who choose their services (translation: when their constituents feel moved to need God).

But let's be clear. I am not a chaplain. I am a pastor. Unlike a chaplain, a pastor assumes that the people he or she lives with in community are more than situationally interested in Jesus. A pastor will comfort. But a pastor will also seek to remind parishioners that all of life is fertile territory for the Spirit's work. A pastor will confront shoddy stewardship and inattention to New Testament disciplines. A pastor will uncover something about a parishioner's prayer life, passions, and hopes for spiritual growth before walking into her hospital room. And yet I think my friend is basically right. Most parishioners want a chaplain rather than a pastor. At least in my experience that's the way they behave. In an age of individualism, most people really don't want someone who reminds, confronts, or uncovers.

In short, it's easy to want chapel and not church. A chapel is a functional place where religious services like weddings are held. Chapels do serve a purpose. You go there, you gather, you normally speak holy words in a sea of secular mishmash. Fine. But let's be clear. Chapel is not church. Not even close. To be faithful to the word *church* requires relinquishment of our agenda and a holy embracing of the Spirit's leading. It means that we will know the teachings of Jesus and seek to bring our lives into concert with his. It means that our lives will be marked with prayer, study, and service. A chaplain will never hound anyone about this. A pastor will. Sadly, most Christians prefer attending chapel rather than being church together. And we've got a bunch of burned-out chaplains trying to fulfill their calling as pastors.

Our family recently hosted a high school German exchange student, Lukas (curiously, the same name as our son), for a month in our home. A young girl at the school became infatuated with Lukas, much to his chagrin. I asked him about the predicament. He shook his head and sadly said, "There is no *soloootion*" (imagine something like California Governor Arnold's Austrian accent here). Our family became fond of using this declaration in response to a variety of challenges in daily life.

In parish ministry, pastors are confronted with problems for which there seem to be no solution—halfhearted commitments, childish behavior, various infidelities, and the cultural embrace of a competing narrative that has little to do with the gospel. But Christ offers a clear solution: to tell the truth so artfully and consistently that we all experience a lifelong series of little deaths and resurrections, nothing short of true conversion to this odd man we know as Savior of the world. His hope and truth echo through the ages: "Beloved, I pray that all may go well with you and that you may be in good health, just as it is well with your soul. I was overjoyed when some of the friends arrived and testified to your faithfulness to the truth, namely how you walk in the truth. I have no greater joy than this, to hear that my children are walking in the truth" (3 John 1:2–4).

You shall know the truth.

And the truth shall make you odd.

Notes

Introduction Quivering Masses of Availability

1. Stanley Hauerwas (Duke Divinity School) derisively uses this phrase to describe pastors whose main goal is always to keep everything smooth and everyone happy in parish life.

2. See Frank G. Honeycutt, *Sanctified Living: More than Grace and Forgiveness* (Minneapolis: Augsburg Fortress, 2008), 34–38.

3. Sissela Bok, *Lying: Moral Choice in Public and Private Life* (New York: Pantheon Books, 1978), 18.

4. Cited in William H. Willimon, *Pastor: The Theology and Practice of Ordained Ministry* (Nashville: Abingdon, 2002), 97.

Chapter 1 Reflections on the Father of Lies

1. Bok, *Lying*, 4.

2. Carl Hiaasen, *Skinny Dip* (New York: Warner Books, 2004), 85.

3. Martin E. Marty, "Heaven and Hell," *The Lutheran*, July 1993, 14–17.

4. Tobias Wolff, "Awake," *The New Yorker*, August 25, 2008, 67.

5. Andrew Delbanco, *The Death of Satan: How Americans Have Lost the Sense of Evil* (New York: Farrar, Strauss & Giroux, 1995), 3, 9.

6. I'll return to the power of faithful catechesis in a later chapter.

7. James Robertson, *The Testament of Gideon Mack* (New York: Viking Press, 2007), 282. You'll love this novel by a Scottish writer not well known in the United States. It's in paperback now; go buy it.

8. Ibid., 283.

9. Ibid., 295.

10. From a news report in the *New York Times*, March 6, 2007.

11. R. T. Smith, "Charlene Sperry on Safe Beauty," in *The Hollow Log Lounge* (Champaign, IL: University of Illinois Press, 2003), 7.

12. Odd name to be associated with a wildfire, please note.

13. Mike Cherney, "Who Is to Blame for Starting Fire?" *Columbia (SC) State*, April 25, 2009, A4.

14. C. S. Lewis, *The Screwtape Letters* (New York: Bantam Books, 1982), 7.

15. "Holy Baptism," *Lutheran Book of Worship* (Minneapolis: Augsburg, 1978), 123.

16. See especially: Ansgar Kelly Henry, *The Devil at Baptism: Ritual, Theology, and Drama* (Ithaca, NY: Cornell University Press, 1985); and Maxwell E. Johnson, *The Rites of Christian Initiation: Their Evolution and Interpretation* (Collegeville, MN: Liturgical Press, 1999).

17. Johnson, *Rites of Christian Initiation*, 95.

18. Scott Peck, *People of the Lie: The Hope for Healing Human Evil* (New York: Simon & Schuster, 1983), 183.

19. Ibid., 185–86.

20. Much of the following section first appeared (in slightly different form) in Frank G. Honeycutt, "Seen and Unseen: On Tardiness and Trust," *The Lutheran*, September 2009, 44–45. Used with permission.

21. Quoted in Annie Dillard, *For the Time Being* (New York: Alfred A. Knopf, 1999), 39.

22. Luci Shaw, "Ghostly," in *Writing the River* (Colorado Springs: Pinon Press), 37.

23. First Corinthians 12:4–13; Romans 12:6–8; Ephesians 4:11–13.

24. The "I" (introversion) explains my behavior waiting for the doctor in the introduction. The "T" (thinking) explains much of my weirdness in this chapter. The "J" (judging) explains why I can seem like an overbearing ass at times.

25. The center deals mostly with polygraph research and the like, but I love the name anyway. Thanks to Helen Doerpinghaus (friend and University of South Carolina professor) for introducing me to their website.

26. Flannery O'Connor, *Wise Blood* (New York: Farrar, Straus & Giroux, 1949), 165.

27. Interesting that Scott Peck defines love this way in *The Road Less Traveled* (New York: Simon & Schuster), 81. "The will to extend one's self for the purpose of nurturing one's own or another's spiritual growth."

Chapter 2 The Lie of Express Conversion

1. Ann McElligott, ed., *The Catechumenal Process: Adult Initiation and Formation for Christian Life and Ministry* (New York: Church Hymnal Corporation, 1990), 1.

2. I always like to remind people that it's not really clear exactly how long Philip lingered in the eunuch's chariot. See Acts 8:29–31—could have been a couple days spent in catechesis. I offer this only partly tongue-in-cheek!

3. See Luke 8:9–10.

4. Garret Keizer, "Reasons to Join," *The Christian Century*, April 22, 2008, 30.

5. John Alexander, "On Becoming an Apache, Part 2," *The Other Side* (January–February 1999): 35.

6. Homer, *The Odyssey*, trans. Robert Fitzgerald (New York: Anchor Books, 1963), 368. I'm indebted to William H. Willimon for pointing out this story from Homer.

7. The two paragraphs prior to this footnote (in slightly different form) are taken from Frank G. Honeycutt, "Living by the Word," *The Christian Century*, April 7, 2009, 19.

8. My dad's grandfather.

9. Ruth Gaines Honeycutt, *A Search for Yesterday*, 21. Privately published by my mother after years of genealogical research in locales including Little Rock, Salt Lake City, South Georgia, North Carolina, and Germany.

10. For a chilling and powerfully told account of a 1970 murder of a black man killed for simply talking to a white woman in public in Oxford, North Carolina, see Timothy B. Tyson, *Blood Done Sign My Name* (New York: Three Rivers Press, 2004). Tyson (age ten when the crime occurred in his childhood town) is the son of a United Methodist pastor. You will not forget this very moving account.

11. The cartoon is by Jack Ziegler.

12. I need to mention here a book that is by far the best resource I've ever read on teen depression: Gary E. Nelson, *A Relentless Hope: Surviving the Storm of Teen Depression* (Eugene, OR: Cascade, 2007).

13. John Wesley, "The New Birth" (sermon XLV), in *The Works of John Wesley*, vol. VI (Grand Rapids: Zondervan, 1972), 65, italics in original.

14. Gordon T. Smith, *Beginning Well: Christian Conversion and Authentic Transformation* (Downers Grove, IL: InterVarsity, 2001), 154.

15. Ibid., 24.

16. Ibid., 24–25.

17. Garrison Keillor, *Pontoon* (New York: Penguin, 2007), 124–25.

18. Again, all names and identifying characteristics have been altered to protect confidentiality. Specific characteristics have been used only with prior consent of the individual. The quotations from this section are from spiritual autobiographies written by participants and used here with permission.

19. Todd Shy, "Recovering Evangelical: Reflections of an Erstwhile Christ Addict," *Image* 51 (Fall 2006): 93.

20. Here I'll list only three: Samuel Torvend and Lani Willis, eds., *Welcome to Christ: A Lutheran Introduction to the Catechumenate* (Minneapolis: Augsburg Fortress, 1997); McElligott, ed., *Catechumenal Process* and Daniel T. Benedict Jr., *Come to the Waters: Baptism and Our Ministry of Welcoming Seekers and Making Disciples* (Nashville: Discipleship Resources, 1996).

21. Our own local version of the catechumenate includes longtime church members who feel a need for additional catechesis and maturation in discipleship.

22. It is possible at this point that group members could be matched with participants from earlier years. I'm aware of one congregation in which a seventeen-year-old baptized at Easter the previous spring became a sponsor for a forty-five-year-old entering the process the following fall.

23. Darrel L. Guder, *The Continuing Conversion of the Church* (Grand Rapids: Eerdmans, 2000), 173.

24. Karl Barth, "The Strange New World within the Bible," in *A Map of Twentieth Century Theology: Readings from Karl Barth to Radical Pluralism*, ed. Carl Braaten and Robert Jenson (Minneapolis: Augsburg Fortress, 1995), 21–31.

25. Guder, *Continuing Conversion*, 163.

26. Frank G. Honeycutt, "The Lure of Express Conversion," in *What Do You Seek? Welcoming the Adult Inquirer* (Minneapolis: Augsburg Fortress, 2000), 16.

Chapter 3 Honesty in Preaching

1. David Bartlett, "Preaching the Truth," in *But Is It All True? The Bible and the Question of* Truth, ed. Alan G. Padgett and Patrick R. Keifert (Grand Rapids: Eerdmans, 2006), 129.

2. Quote taken from the church newsletter *The Messenger of Faith Lutheran Church* (Lexington, KY), Ronald G. Luckey, pastor.

3. I love the Greek here: "in a riddle."

4. Thomas G. Long, "Stolen Goods: Tempted to Plagiarize," *The Christian Century*, April 17, 2007, 20.

5. I'll not name the publisher here, but a friend refers to this company as "the mangy dog of Christian publishing."

6. Long, "Stolen Goods," 18.

7. Ibid., 21.

8. See Numbers 1:46—surely an inflated figure, but the number still points to the spiritual sagacity and holy temperament of Moses.

9. Flannery O'Connor, *Wise Blood* (New York: Farrar, Straus & Giroux, 1984), 113.

10. Michael Rogness, "More than Good Theology," *Word and World* 19, no. 1 (Winter 1999): 68.

11. Ron Luckey is pastor of Faith Lutheran Church in Lexington, Kentucky. The date of this email is April 9, 2009. Used with permission.

12. Marilynne Robinson, *Gilead* (New York: Farrar, Straus & Giroux, 2004), 70.

13. I'm honestly open to other interpretations of this confusing Exodus passage. Contact me through our church website (www.ebenezerlutheran.org) if you have alternate ideas.

14. Thomas G. Long, *Preaching from Memory to Hope* (Louisville: Westminster John Knox, 2009), 20.

15. Bartlett, "Preaching the Truth," 124.

16. The correct answers in order are C, B, A, D, E.

17. Ron Rash, "Under Jocassee," in *Raising the Dead* (Oak Ridge, TN: Iris Press, 2002), 4.

18. M. Craig Barnes, *The Pastor as Minor Poet: Texts and Subtexts in the Ministerial Life* (Grand Rapids: Eerdmans, 2009), 125, 130.

19. Roger Rosenblatt, "Making Toast," *The New Yorker*, December 15, 2008, 45.

20. Annie Dillard, *For the Time Being* (New York: Knopf, 1999), 166–67.

21. John Piper, "The President, the Passengers, and the Patience of God," January 21, 2009. The essay may be found at Piper's website, www.desiringgod.org.

22. Ron Hansen, "The Sparrow," *Image* 60 (Winter 2008–9): 7–14.

23. Ibid., 11.

24. Ibid., 13.

25. Ibid., 14.

26. Tracy Kidder, *Mountains beyond Mountains* (New York: Random House, 2004), 85.

27. Long, *Preaching from Memory to Hope*, 21–22.

Chapter 4 Truth and Consequences in Pastoral Care

1. Martin B. Copenhaver, "Handshake Ritual: Ministry at the Church Door," *The Christian Century*, April 8, 2008, 25.

2. Bill Bryson, *The Life and Times of the Thunderbolt Kid: A Memoir* (New York: Broadway, 2006), 63.

3. Some commentators believe it would have been culturally impossible to have had five husbands in first-century Samaritan life due to biblical law. Given the proximity to the wedding at Cana in chapter 2 of John, these same scholars see *husband* figuratively as an idol that takes the place of one's true Lord. I like this interpretation but still say Jesus has it in him to be overtly rude and confrontational.

4. Yes, I'm aware that six is the imperfect biblical number. I daresay, however, that Jesus wasn't hoping for a seventh man in this woman's life (unless perhaps it was him as Lord). Check out the very amusing book of Tobit (especially chapters 7 and 8) for an entertaining tale of a woman who had seven husbands and only found marital bliss with her eighth. The first seven die in the very act of sexual congress, prompting the eighth (Tobias) to offer the first prayer for safe sex in 8:5–8.

5. Barnes, *Pastor as Minor Poet*, 92.

6. Ibid., 9: "Reflective pastors will often attempt to defend against all of these projected identities by looking deep into their hearts and asking, 'Who do I think I am?' But our hearts are also conflicted. Even if we succeed in drawing into our hearts, it usually feels like a bad committee meeting is going on in there—so many internalized voices are vying for attention and trying to hijack the agenda."

7. John Updike, *A Month of Sundays* (Greenwich, CT: Fawcett Publications, 1974), 9–10.

8. Walter E. Wiest and Elwyn A. Smith, *Ethics in Ministry: A Guide for the Professional* (Minneapolis: Fortress, 1990), 21–22.

9. Richard Lischer, *Open Secrets: A Memoir of Faith and Discovery* (New York: Broadway, 2001), 115.

10. Greg Williams, "Crash: On the Corner of 34th and Park, Three Lives Changed Forever," *New York Times*, September 27, 2004.

11. Eugene Peterson, *Working the Angles: The Shape of Pastoral Integrity* (Grand Rapids: Eerdmans, 1987), 15.

12. David Guterson, *Our Lady of the Forest* (New York: Knopf, 2003), 63–64. There are no quotation marks in the original.

13. Peterson, *Working the Angles*, 18.

14. Philip Yancey, *Reaching for the Invisible God: What Can We Expect to Find?* (Grand Rapids: Zondervan, 2000), 88.

15. C. S. Lewis, *The Silver Chair* (New York: Macmillan, 1953), 158–59.

16. A footnote in my Bible calls this "insania zoanthropia," a form of mental illness "in which a man acts like a beast." Not a bad diagnosis for much of what ails us in the twenty-first century.

Chapter 5 Truthful Teaching

1. Dallas Willard, *The Divine Conspiracy: Rediscovering Our Hidden Life in God* (San Francisco: HarperCollins, 1998), 307.

2. See Willard, *The Divine Conspiracy*, 350. "Paul's letter to the Colossians is perhaps the best overall statement on the spiritual formation of the disciple in the New Testament. I suspect this is because it was written to people whom Paul had never met and had never had the opportunity to teach."

3. See my book on sanctification from a Lutheran perspective: Honeycutt, *Sanctified Living*.

4. See chapter 2 and my comments on the catechumenal process.

5. L. Gregory Jones, "Embodying Scripture in the Community of Faith," in *The Art of Reading Scripture*, ed. Ellen F. Davis and Richard B. Hays (Grand Rapids: Eerdmans, 2003), 145.

6. Ibid.

7. Nica Lalli, "No Religion? No Problem," *USA Today*, April 6, 2009, 15A.

8. Sam Harris, *Letter to a Christian Nation* (New York: Vintage, 2006), xi–xii, italics original.

9. Ibid., 105.

10. See Barbara Brown Taylor, "Tales of Terror, Times of Wonder," *The Other Side* (March–April 2000): 14–17. "The Bible is not simply a book about admirable people or even about a conventionally admirable God. Instead it is a book about a sovereign God's covenant with a chosen people, as full of holy terrors as it is of holy wonders, none of which we may avoid without avoiding part of the truth" (14).

11. For example, during week three of our class, an article about a woman in Spartanburg seeing the face of Jesus in a piece of cheese toast appeared on the front page of a major section of our local paper: Lee G. Healy, "Manna from Heaven? Jesus Is in the Eye of the Beholder," *Columbia (SC) State*, April 23, 2009, B1. We watched during this class a clip from Bill Maher's documentary *Religulous*. Maher has a field day with such people.

Chapter 6 Death and Deceit

1. Quoted in Annie Dillard, *For the Time Being* (New York: Alfred A. Knopf, 1999), 75.

2. Mark Twain, "Buck Fanshaw's Funeral," in *The Complete Short Stories of Mark Twain*, ed. Charles Neider (New York: Bantam, 1978), 70.

3. William H. Willimon, "Accidental Lessons: My Encounter with a Chainsaw," *The Christian Century*, April 21, 2009, 31.

4. Chet Raymo, *The Soul of the Night: An Astronomical Pilgrimage* (Cambridge, MA: Cowley, 1992), 3.

5. Steve Martin, "Side Effects," *The New Yorker*, April 13, 1998, 84.

Fhojan!

6. Christine Montross, *Body of Work: Meditations on Mortality from the Human Anatomy Lab* (New York: Penguin Books, 2007), 36.

7. Richard John Neuhaus, *The Eternal Pity* (Notre Dame, IN: University of Notre Dame Press, 2000), 2.

8. Melissa Chappell, excerpt from her unpublished poem, "It is all that I can do." Used with permission.

9. Michael Heher, "Words to Match," *Image*, no. 23 (Summer 1999): 102.

10. Thomas Lynch, *Bodies in Motion and at Rest: On Metaphor and Mortality* (New York: W.W. Norton, 2001), 96: "The effort to minimize the hurt by minimizing the loss, pretending that a dead body has lost its meaning or identity, is another tune we whistle past the graveyard."

11. Nicholas Wolterstorff, *Lament for a Son* (Grand Rapids: Eerdmans, 1987), 34.

12. For a very helpful discussion of this old, misunderstood doctrine, see Rodney Clapp, *Tortured Wonders: Christian Spirituality for People, Not Angels* (Grand Rapids: Brazos, 2004), 25–48.

13. Rodney Clapp, "Blest Be the Ties That Bind," *The Christian Century*, May 5, 2009, 61.

14. Ron Rash, *Saints at the River* (New York: Henry Holt, 2004), 5.

15. C. S. Lewis, *The Voyage of the Dawn Treader* (New York: Macmillan, 1952), 90.

16. Elizabeth Strout, "Incoming Tide," in *Olive Kitteridge* (New York: Random House, 2008), 33.

17. Peter De Vries, *The Blood of the Lamb* (New York: Little, Brown, 1961), 238.

18. Annie Dillard, *The Living* (New York: HarperCollins, 1992), 63.

19. Thomas Lynch, *The Undertaking: Life Studies from the Dismal Trade* (New York: Penguin, 1997), 46.

20. Ibid., 51.

21. Confession: my usual seat exactly.

22. Cited in Kathleen Norris, *The Cloister Walk* (New York: Riverhead, 1996), 204.

23. Peter W. Marty, "Holding Steady: The Nonanxious Pastor," *The Christian Century*, April 5, 2003, 9.

Chapter 7 Remaining in Ephesus

1. Barbara Brown Taylor, "The Perfect Mirror," *The Christian Century*, March 18–25, 1998, 283.

2. Walter Brueggemann, "Truth-Telling as Subversive Obedience," in *The Word Militant* (Minneapolis: Fortress, 2008), 175.

3. William Willimon, "On the Attack with Jesus" (Yost Lectures, Lutheran Theological Southern Seminary, Columbia, SC, May 14, 2009).

4. Ibid.

5. Harry Emerson Fosdick, "Making the Best of a Bad Mess," in *The Hope of the World: Twenty-Five Sermons on Christianity Today* (New York: Harper & Brothers, 1933), 118.

Conclusion Why Church Members Need More than a Chaplain Who Cares

1. Margaret A. Miller, "Professing Truth(s)," *Change: The Magazine for Higher Learning*, November 20, 2008.

2. Peterson, *Working the Angles*, 5.

3. Thomas G. Long, *Testimony: Talking Ourselves into Being Christian* (San Francisco: Jossey-Bass, 2004), 99.

4. See the very amusing and wise article by Walter Kirn, "The Autumn of the Multitaskers," *Atlantic*, November 2007, 66–80.

5. Neil Postman, *Amusing Ourselves to Death: Public Discourse in the Age of Show Business* (New York: Penguin Books, 1986), 44–45.